THINKING OF SKINS

CAROL RUMENS

Thinking of Skins

NEW & SELECTED POEMS

BLOODAXE BOOKS

ISBN: 1 85224 280 9   humca

First published 1993 by
Bloodaxe Books Ltd,
P.O. Box 1SN,
Newcastle upon Tyne NE99 1SN.

Bloodaxe Books Ltd acknowledges
the financial assistance of Northern Arts.

Cover printing by J. Thomson Colour Printers Ltd, Glasgow.

Printed in Great Britain by
Cromwell Press Ltd, Broughton Gifford, Melksham, Wiltshire.

For Edna Longley

Acknowledgements

Many of these poems were written during the various residencies I have held over the last decade, and I would like to thank the Universities of Kent, Newcastle and Durham, and Queen's University, Belfast, as well as the Arts Councils of Great Britain and Northern Ireland, and Northern Arts. I am grateful to the current members of the creative writing groups at Queen's for the stimulus of their commitment and enthusiasm, and I would especially like to thank Alan Hollinghurst, for being, over the years, a perceptive and loyal poetry editor.

The poems in the second part of this book are selected from the following collections: *A Strange Girl in Bright Colours* (Quartet Books, 1973), *Unplayed Music* (Secker & Warburg, 1981), *Star Whisper* (Secker & Warburg, 1983), *Direct Dialling* (Chatto & Windus, 1985), *Icons, Waves* (Starwheel Press, 1986), *Selected Poems* (Chatto & Windus, 1987), *The Greening of the Snow Beach* (Bloodaxe Books, 1988) and *From Berlin to Heaven* (Chatto & Windus, 1989).

Acknowledgements are due to the editors of the following publications in which some of the new poems first appeared (not necessarily in a final version): *Ambit, Aquarius, Exposure, Fortnight, The Honest Ulsterman, The Independent on Sunday, Irish Review, Marathon Anthology, Oxford Magazine, The Poetry Book Society Anthology 1989-1990* (PBS/Hutchinson, 1989), *The Poetry Book Society Anthology 2 & 3* (PBS/Hutchinson, 1991 & 1992), *Poetry Ireland, Poetry Review, Poetry Wales, The Rialto, The Times Literary Supplement, Ulster Newsletter, Windows* and *Writing Ulster*.

Contents

AUTHOR'S NOTE

Thinking of Skins falls, broadly speaking, into two parts. The first consists of new poems, written, roughly between 1989 and 1993; the second is a selection which revises, and, I hope, re-focuses the *Selected Poems* published by Chatto in 1987. It adds the sequence *Icons, Waves* (Starwheel Press, 1986) as well as poems from *The Greening of the Snow Beach* (Bloodaxe, 1988) and *From Berlin to Heaven* (Chatto, 1989). This second part spans published work from my early twenties to my early forties. I have resisted the temptation to add any unpublished material from that time.

Many of the later poems in the first part of the book were written in Belfast. They should not be searched for my opinions about Northern Ireland, nor for any would-be objective statement about "the situation" here. "My" Belfast is a muse-city, a city of weather and uncertainty. If my settings are more likely to contain trees than barbed wire, this is because I am lucky enough to know first-hand the leafier aspect of Belfast. It is not the whole story, far from it, but it is not a lie. And I do not offer it to the reader in complete political innocence. I want to show a city where, in spite of everything, peace, love, friends and poems are sometimes made, and where a female imagination can find mirrors, because there is a widespread assumption elsewhere that these things do not exist, that there is only the endless, intolerable round of horror. At the same time, I don't want to minimise this horror or suggest that anyone is not touched by it. Time will no doubt sweep me away soon, so I publish these new poems as my greeting to Belfast and my valediction, should valediction prove inevitable. This is something I have felt in the many different places where I have lived for the past ten years. Perhaps it is this uncertainty of location, this instability of the ground beneath me (which feels so insistently like home) that is responsible, as well as sheer ignorance of course, for the lack of focus, or the peculiar focus, in the work. I hope it will be forgiven by those who know the city far better than I ever will, and who are chronicling it in the depth and complexity it deserves.

CAROL RUMENS
Belfast, September 1993

'It is easier to die than to remember.'

BASIL BUNTING
Briggflatts

THINKING OF SKINS
(1993)

Until We Could Hardly See Them

It was the living who took offence
At our elegies, our desire
To find out, to make amends.
They called it appropriation.
They said we were the wrong race or religion.
Borders and ghettoes held like knots in their hearts
And shortened their memories.
They should have asked the dead before they judged us.

Whoever tries to imagine them
Comforts them, the dead,
Who have learned they are simply children,
So must one day be abandoned.
Now they cry from the middle of the road,
Stop, please, stop, take us with you.
We don't weigh much, we won't take up much room.
They are glad of any hand,
Even one whose flesh is scented with luck,
And any voice that names them
– Never mind our bad pronunciation –
Warms the great silence they bear.
They smile, they stretch their fingers
To touch our cheeks. They say we take after them.
They say we're their living image
And indeed we will be, that day
We ask nothing more of the future,
Only not to be left like shadows on the road
Where so many became no one.

St Petersburg, Reclaimed by Merchants

The wind was terrorising the simple river,
Smacking the wobbly flesh about its waist-band.
Pushkin, the tourists thought, looking tenderly down
At the curled green lip, the slurping meal.
The locals stared at a different kind of moral.
Flood was a long word in a poem they'd learned
At school. Now they were learning grown-up things:
How much to ask for a papier mâché icon
Stolen by someone's cousin, how not to be sold
Down the metaphorical river, and other secrets
Dark as the dark-eyed bride the match-maker brings.

A Prophet, Unhonoured
(for Jan Kavan)

Eloquence, irony and lying low
– These were your gifts, the gifts of opposition.
I hope they're proving useful to you now,
As when I learned the fine points of your mission
In London, back in '82 and '3.
Your neighbours, it turned out, were qualified
For jobs in Husak's State Security.
They asked me if I worked for you. I said
I was your girlfriend. (But I never was.)
They shopped you to the Council, all the same:
Your crime, running a business from your place
Of residence – a very English crime.
An investigator called. We buzzed him in
('The lift's gone wrong, you'll have to use the stairs!')
And flew about, got every damned machine
Bundled away, toys strewn, said a few prayers.
Your daughter's absence filled the room. He guessed
Perhaps, but chose to leave the signs unread.

We made a sort of family: Brits, obsessed
With 'freedom', Czechs, hard-boiled in Prague street-cred.
Arrests and disappearance, beatings, rape
– The bad news had its ways of twisting through.
You'd spell the names for me, place accents, keep
Them talking, simply telling what they knew.
You *lived in truth*, I think, but not in hate.
(Is this why some have struck you off their list?)
You thought it worthwhile, arguing with a state
Which might still earn its title, Socialist.
For that, we'd work the night away, my longhand
Struggling with obsolescence as you schemed
And sped the filthy era to its end.
Your passage home was earned, not merely dreamed.
So was the revolution 'velvet', new
And candle-soft? Or did it win its rough
First shape from the patient realists, like you,
Working with slipperier, more dangerous stuff
– Jan Palach's last handclasp, the ink-soaked type
In use before the new technology,
Back in the days when innocence, like sleep,
Was one more spurious foreign luxury?

NOTE: After promising the dying Jan Palach to continue to fight for democratic
socialism, Jan Kavan, exiled in London, founded and ran Palach Press. This
was a news agency dedicated to informing the media about the activities of the
Czech dissident movement, Charta 77, and publishing its own regular Bulletin.
Kavan returned to Prague after the political changes, but according to reports
in the British press, has since been severely criticised for previous collaboration
with the State. The poem simply affirms my sense of the honest idealism with
which Kavan worked in the days when I was a part-time assistant at Palach
Press. *Living in the Truth* is the title of a book by Vaclav Havel.

Seascape and Single Figure

It isn't the seagulls, whitened
Lecterns of rock or wind,
Whose cries make the heart cry,
But those who scatter delinquent
Footprints, feathered with sand,
As the visible evidence that children fly.

My shadow, askance and pale,
Crosses the beach with me:
We sit on the spread towel,
Folded together complicatedly
As a marriage or Swiss Army knife.
So the shadow is one with the life.

Nearby, a village is settled
With windbreaks, push-chairs.
Children gather and build.
The candid embodiment of
The most popular version of love,
They are the day's, its flush, its goldening, theirs.

And disinheritance
Is the sea, burnt almost to nothing,
A chemical, austere,
Standoffish radiance
Sending a few thin waves, slow-lathering,
Choked, to encrust the shore.

What does it matter if less
Than a dazzled moment ago
I swam with the warmer flow?
Those choices, that lack of choice,
That enviable sorrow,
Are not renewable.

Bright as crayoned sunshine, still
The coast-train winds among
The drifted crowds, pouring them out like grain
From a summer which, for so long
Disguised as a miracle,
Empties only to fill and brim again.

Walking Out

Walking out on them would be like this,
She'd always known: the feeling of pretence
As she strolled on and on (she could go back
Any time, even now), the shore-lights drilling
Through scrambled pinks and blues the inky block
Of river (or she could jump in and drown),
The thrill of reading from a bland tin sign
She'd stepped across a border, changed her town
(But even so, she could go back). And then
The hunger, deepening till she called it hers.
She crossed towards a blare of infra-red
Announcing the Monster Burger, the Special Grill,
And took her place, and thanked the hand that fed.
There was another room, half in darkness:
She couldn't work out what was going on
– The disco sex-thud, squealing playground voices –
Until she saw the cake float by, frilled skirt
And seven shivering haloes. Then she cut
One more smashed mouthful, pushed away her plate.
This was how it was too, she might have known:
Whichever way you walked, their mugger's eyes
Shone at you. They didn't want your life.
They wanted everything you'd planned to give them
Before you knew you had no choice beyond
The choice that gave them birth. Birth was your crime,
And after that all innocence was gone.
At the till she waved a dirty five-pound note
–Not for the children's childhood, but her own.

Last of the Lays

Part One

At Ivalo's tyre-crazed cross-roads, snow was the sphinx
And *Murmansk* was what she murmured. One night you got restless.

(The nights were long, alas. We weren't new lovers.
'Follow me. I am your Fate' wouldn't wash any more).

I heard your foot-swords slicing the forest-fleece
With finality. Then from your breast swooped a brilliant birdman.

Choice, choice, choice gasped the wind as you gashed it.
In front of you, ghostly as lilacs, stood your live lungs.

Part Two

In Persil-white Ivalo the enemy was drink.
I had nothing to come to but a Finnish Cosmo

And nothing to read but a radioactive omelette.
My cutlery stuttered, my skis would begin any minute,

So I tacked outside into a mean minus-thirty,
And wound up at the Word, that high-lettered horror.

I turned as it told me. I plummeted and plodged
And became wild-life and expected instant extinction.

I lit on the luminous secret of synchronised movement
Momentarily, but omitted to take it with me.

I slept on my skis, and revolutionary roughnecks
Lobbed snow-lumps like one-off hand-jobs, and roamed the ice

Like spinning-tops wreathed in a frost of eye-water.

Part Three

Bang on the border, they'd opened a Super-Safeways,
Hit by recession, closed for the duration.

Some tanked-up gun-jabber jogged me: 'Nadezhda Krupskaya?'
'Crumbs!' I said. 'Wrong revolution. Julian Clary.'

Part Four

He didn't find that funny, which meant, as I'd feared,
History hadn't happened, it hadn't begun.

And though the ski-tracks still straggled under the *Push* sign
They were being disexisted at serious speed.

This was the hairiest I had ever imagined:
Me, on God's side, just about. You, back on the other:

The border, bristling. Remember those terrible games
– When the sound's switched off, there's got to be someone dancing,

And the grin's de rigeur, because English losers are laughers?
I hope, wherever you're harboured, you look like a natural

– Straight bck, heels tgthr, bm on chr –
I hope when it thaws and the home-thoughts unfreeze our faces,

Whoever I am I'll
                    author an honest tear.

The Muse of Argument

At first, no more than
   A fret of breeze that twists
The fossil bracken,
   Shyness and anger twin-
Leashed to a straining wrist:
   Then she is visible
And she embodies all
   Silence that steels itself
Under a woman's heartbeat
   And stammers to take aim.
I keep back my breath
   For her, but the dart has skimmered
Already, sealed its roost
   In disarray: the sky
Plunges, heels alight
   And tightly pressed.
Plaudits, abasements die
   At her feet, with clouded looks.
And still she seems to doubt
   Her own connection.
Her shoulders are a book,
   Caught naked, trying to close,
And her face has taken on
   The colour of a wound,
   Its deep, historic rose.

Dreams of Revolution

She's walking somewhere unresolved, sea-ravished,
Taking the flesh-tints of the facing sky
Among the stones, distributing them in water
Because there are no poor, now, in the village.

This is her lover's name-delighted class-room.
His finger prints a chalk-rose on her wrist
And leads her eyes to where a migrant shimmer
Of cursive vanishes on the rinsed slate.

He doesn't mind her townee misconceptions.
He scarcely knows the drift of his own arm
– Whether or not it lodges on her shoulder:
All her dear world's his habitat, and habit.

And this machine contracts them both, so perfect,
One stolen berry means a night of storms
And flight scattered next day in lumps and meltings
Of slashed upholstery, as if the sky

Had tried to move, and failed. Nothing moves freely
Here but the sea, old and unreconstructed.
It drowns the clover, mocks the poor, entices
Love's great protection-racket to its housing.

In the Season of Green Gowns

Summer will take from you everything I desire:
It will pluck at your sleeve, quietly undo
A handful of buttons, seeking no disclosure
That wasn't first fully consented to,
As you walked and turned in your mirror's candid gaze
And wouldn't be rushed. Summer, shyly approving,
Will lead you from chaste decision to easy living.

Summer will tell me what I could never enquire:
The pale length of your arm, sleeved in its years,
The freckled blush at the wrist. Summer confirms
The less-than-perfect as our most tender haunting.
It pours my desire into the depth of the mould
Like a conception. But, like a man or a child,
I simply can't tell if you are filled or wanting.

The Impenitent

The wife of the poet can't be innocent
Her eyes must be narrow
The wife of the poet can't be humble
She must lift her chin high
The wife of the poet won't be flattered
If he writes a poem in her blood
The wife of the poet knows the missing word
But she'll never tell him.

The husband of the poet can't be light-hearted
He must watch the pennies
The husband of the poet can't be clean
He must live in his dust
The husband of the poet can't be original
He must be, or obey, her muse
The husband of the poet knows the missing word
And that it's '*wife*'.

The Last Wife's Consolation

When his body grew tired of hers, she knew there was no solution.
He had never seen her young, so he lacked that particular image
To gloss over her blemishes, to kiss in her unlit eyes.
She looked in the mirror, and nothing there entranced her:
On the other hand, she had never been honey and bright new milk
– And maybe his body's tiredness had nothing to do with her,
And maybe not even her youth could have been the beautiful cure.

The Colouring Age

Like a shower of red rain
    Blown across the wall
Of that suburban garden
    Where sense is made of all
That's rampant, archetypal,
    The hawthorn sails again
Into her colouring-age,
    Her knack is effortless
But might discourage
    Those for whom spring's good news
Is getting worse.
    Moans in the quiet night
Could equally be the dryad
    Bled by a vandal
To pulp, or the deferred
    Grief of the gardenless
Ex-suburbanite
    Acknowledging a loss.

Ghosts never cease to pull
    On a woman's wrists,
Beg to be carried, still,
    At twenty-plus.
They're all ventriloquists
    Hurtling their voices
From each secluded lawn;
    And she will always turn,
Being an expert on love,
    Burdened by sheer talent.
O trees, O pavement,
    O things that never move,
Tell her how to live
    With no doorstep to stand on.
Each doorbell lately pressed
    Had lost its tongue.
None that she ever kissed
    Could bear it for very long.

This flowering tree invites
     Her to go under,
Suffer the pains and lights
     That prove the wonder
Of modern physics which
     Disprove the clock.
Forward is really back.
     There's no other to get-out
From the whole silly story
     But to unravel, stitch
By stitch the contrived plot,
     Downsliding all the way
To that beginning,
     That once-upon-a-time,
She'd pitched her life to swing
     A million miles from:

Home. And what is home
     But to be thirteen
And mocked, for ever,
     Your love, a crush; your dream,
A different mother?
     Nothing in your garden
Is quite inanimate
     And that deep-blushing tree
Your father slashes down
     With incomprehensible hate,
Has certainly been hurt.
     Hawthorn blossom's unlucky,
The wise folk say.
     You mount an artistic
Rescue-operation
     Boldly, any way,
Lift armfuls of it in,
     And scrape persistently
With crumbling pastels
     Until the paper's skin
Breaks into leaves again
     And the heat of petals,
Forgetting while you can
     That the dark grass outside
Had seemed to float in blood
     – And that blood, your own.

Prelapsarian

Glassy spittle shot all over our windscreen
As we arrived, but the bevy of hook-shaped birds
Swaying towards us, bluer than any storm-cloud,
Was a different proposition, an augury
That seemed benevolent. The donkeys watched
From sly, archaic eyes, but we were careful,
Treading the frosted ladder to our high
Loft, and I was careful every morning.
Though always thrilled with the first splash of flight
That drenched the trees in blue, I came down slowly,
Forcing both my hands round the scalding rails.
There would be mountains to climb, the hips and noses
Of lightly-sleeping giants, and Christmas Eve
We would remember the distant births of children:
Otherwise, though naked, we seemed blameless.

When we held out dark jewels of Christmas pudding
The jostle of beaks scarcely pricked our palms.
The donkeys wore old velvet, hung their heads
In an extreme of patience, almost satire,
Knowing the world is paddock grass, that apples
Don't grow on trees, they let us offer them
Our cores. Their soft black-tulip mouths were smiling.

Green Love

To watch you is to watch some other species
Going about its life, a graceful expert,
Unaltered by the passion of my study.
For how much longer? How can I be withheld?

Can I, by taking thought, subtract one image
That made these eyes confederates of your heaven,
Find the small places where wings became leaf-mould, where
A god might shed his last human resemblance,
File away love's name in the catalogue
Of skins and brittle forests: let you live?

England to Her Maker

Hephaestus we tried to tell you
the signs were everywhere
you kept your head down

face to the glare
hammering bevelling punching
all that noise and smoke

no wonder you didn't hear
you were wreathed in the heat
and darkness of your craft

never stood upright except
to hammer our silences
with ringing cries of grievance

peculiar to your class
eyes clearer than yours Hephaestus
were noting the lack of new orders

we don't deny you had skills
you armed the fighting gods
invented such curiosities

as the self-propelling tripod
the fire-breathing bronze bull
magnificent yet not

exactly what life's about
any more we have microchips
we have genuine automation

quiet machines that can reason
unlike your rough irons
clanking brainlessly filthily

think of your lungs black
as the grass round here your legs
bowed under you like pliers

you could have a job sitting down
somewhere warm and well-lit
where there's music plants fountains

imagine yourself with white cuffs
tapping a keyboard smiling
taking credit-cards only smiling

it's the future you can't fight the future
you can't argue with progress
Hephaestus look at it this way

My Two Muses

The younger would fetch you a slap round the face
And you felt it as the most whimsical caress.

But oh, the caresses of the older girl
Were stinging-nettles shoved into the soul.

One taught me the skin's delight, the other, its pain.
I was in love with both of them at first
But my eyes were opened by the older one
Who said: *don't believe a word my sister says.*

I won't, sweetheart, I swear. I swear I never have done.

Charm Against the Virtuous

There's a phoney cow you think's your friend, but her milk will give
    you rabies.
When you want to play at Mums and Dads, she wants to play
    Mummies and Babies.
And if you're feeling a little bit low, she'll tell you what you need
And she'll give you a couple of Nurofen, but I will give you speed.

She's old as your gran, she's got no man, she's never been out of
    this city.
She's nice as pie but it's all my eye, don't ever swallow her pity.
She wants you soft, she wants you sweet, but you'd better be hard
    and brave.
She'll carry you off to a ceilidh, but I'll give you an all-night rave.

Oh you're the wildest of any of us, I've seen it in your eyes.
You know I know what turns you on and I know you like a surprise.
You've been fucked up and so have I, let's get fucked up some more
And take no shit from that holy cow, but show her the old barn-door.

That Bloody Kid Again

My estranged body came back to me one night.
It said 'Aren't you going to kill the fatted calf?'
'No' I said, 'But sit down, any way.
Not too close, please'. 'Well, have I changed much?'
'No, you were always ugly.' And I smiled
Because, to tell you the truth, in the dimmish light
It looked OK. 'What are you doing these days?'
My estranged body pointed to various marks
On its hands and shins, and grumbled 'Moving house.
I've moved so much I don't know who I am.
I'm always encountering chunks of furniture,
Walls, et cetera, that say I don't exist,
Ovens I haven't got to grips with, burn me.
One day my hair caught fire. It's a miracle
I'm still alive'. 'And yet,' I said, 'You are,'
Hating that note of self-pity in its voice.
There was a long silence. 'What are you thinking?'
'I think I'm bleeding'. 'How original.'
'You couldn't lend me...?' 'No. It's time you went,
Anyway, I'm expecting my lover.'
'How can you make love without a body?'
'I see you're still a megalomaniac.'
My body lurked at the door aggrievedly.
'It's raining'. 'So? You won't be washed away.
Come back when you've grown up. If you ever do.'
'I'd rather die than grow up into you.'

Midnight
(i.m. Jerry Orpwood, 1942-88)

The day was a difficult child.
Now it's fallen asleep,
You can hear yourself breathing
Evenly, without fear.

The emptied hour-glass shines,
Sealing the last room,
The last absence, like a mirror.

Why should you turn it over?

At this moment only
The silver pathway lies
Open at your feet.

It will mount the stairs with you
And unfurl into the stars,
Their distant dream-school.

Stretch your hand to the light-switch,
Press your face among feathers,
The soft pen-nibs scratching
A peaceful nonsense.

Think dizzily of the tilt
Of the world again, the weight:
How its dark sands are massing
To drop another day.

The Lost Language of Birth

To be here, to be nowhere, nervous as the wind
Or the landing-lights at ten thousand feet,
Systole, diastole, hanging by a thread

Over the reticent, brick-humble roads
Which turn their backs on me like men not guilty,
Not going anywhere, their eyes hilly:

To be dropped in my own pocket, my own excuses.
To ripple like a blue pain through the lough,
Mountainous hands arranging the hip-bones wide

For that great loneliness, birth. To walk across carpets
I must have stolen, out of rooms that drain
The heart of colour from my children's faces.

To know which side of the road death lives, yet love
The youngest tones of white, from blush to faintness:
To enter like a girl, pushing lips and elbows

Up into the breathy climate of lycra,
Emerging slicked and open-mouthed, the wild glass
Gaping forbidden words like 'swan', like 'girl'.

The Fuchsia Knight
(for Medbh McGuckian)

You gathered his yarn onto unfamiliar looms,
And the vowels you dropped, the soft-signs you appended,
Brindled the cloth and changed it, like the tears
Forged in the hedgerows, bending the thick stems
With weights not even a god deserves to weep.

You bore him flowers which seemed so abundantly
Indigenous, he forgot his planter's rank.
His head grew misty with heather: luminous roses
And the never-heard song of his native nightingale
Brimmed between him and his sword. He learned to drink

Your consonants with childish intensity
As you chased them towards him with a dry-lipped stammer
Less part of the need for love than the search for perfection.
He learned that to open the veins of speech is sometimes
To unzip the fuchsia linings of live skin.

Stealing the Genre

It was the shortest night of the year. I'd been drinking
But I was quite lucid and calm. So, having seen her
The other side of the bar, shedding her light
On no one who specially deserved it, I got to my feet
And simply went over and asked her, in a low voice,
If she'd come to my bed. She raised her eyebrows strangely
But didn't say 'no'. I went out. I felt her follow.

My mind was a storm as we silently crossed the courtyard
In the moist white chill of the dawn. Dear God, I loved her.
I'd loved her in books, I'd adored her at the first sighting.
But no, I'm a woman, English, not young. How could I?
She'd vanished for years. And now she was walking beside me.
Oh what am I going to do, what are *we* going to do?
Perhaps she'll know. She's probably an old hand
– But this sudden thought was the most disturbing of all.

As soon as we reached my room, though, it was plain
She hadn't a clue. We stood like window-displays
In our dawn-damp suits with the short, straight, hip-hugging skirts
(Our styles are strangely alike, I suppose it's because
Even she has to fight her corner in a man's world)
And discussed the rain, which was coming down, and the view,
Which was nothing much, a fuchsia hedge and some trees,
And we watched each other, as women do watch each other,
And tried not to yawn. Why don't you lie down for a bit?
I whispered, inspired. She gratefully kicked off her shoes.

She was onto the bed in no time, and lay as if dumped
On the furthest edge, her face – dear God – to the wall.
I watched for a while, and, thinking she might be in tears,
Caressed the foam-padded viscose that passed for her shoulder,
And begged her not to feel guilty. Then I discovered
That all she was doing was breathing, dead to the world.

It wasn't an insult, exactly, but it was a let-down
– And yet I admired her. Sleep. If only I could.
I rested my hand at an uncontroversial location
South of her breasts, maybe North, I don't remember,
And ached with desire and regret and rationalisation.

I'd asked her to bed. And she'd come to bed. End of story.
Only it wasn't the story I'd wanted to tell.
Roll on, tomorrow, I urged, but tomorrow retorted:
I'm here already, and nothing ever gets better.

But then, unexpectedly, I began to feel pleased.
To think she was here, at my side, so condensed, so weighty!
In my humble position (a woman, English, not young,
Et cetera) what more could I ask of an Irish dawn
Than this vision, alive, though dead to the world, on my duvet?
What have I done to deserve her? Oh, never mind,
Don't think about words like 'deserve'. So we lay in grace.
The light. Her hair. My hand. Her breath. And the fuchsias.
I thought of the poem I'd write, and fell asleep, smiling.

I woke in a daze of sublime self-congratulation
And saw she was gone. My meadow, my cloud, my aisling!
I could hardly believe my own memory. I wanted to scream
All over the courtyard, come back, come to bed, but how could I?
She might be anywhere, people were thick in the day
Already, and things were normal. Why are things normal?

I keened her name to the walls, I swam bitterest rivers,
I buried my face in the cloth where her blushes had slipped
And left a miraculous print that would baffle the laundry:
Oh let me die now. And the dark was all flame as I drank
The heart-breaking odour of Muguets des Bois and red wine
– Hers, though I have to admit, it could have been mine.

Chippa Rippa
for Elena Seymenliyska

Re-wakened memory-sound: the rustly chip and chock
As the poker rummages: the obedient mutter
And gush of the stirred coal, relinquishing
Its ardent childhood wish – to be immortal.

Variant Readings

I expected bleachworks and burnt-out cars, not fuchsias:
Not cedar and sky-trickling larch, their remote massed shade,
Nor to hear my footsteps, lonely in streets of wet hedges
That tell me: here peace, and love, and money, are made.

Home was like this long ago, but can't be again.
I'll have chosen guilt and illusion, if I choose this
Most English of Irelands, our difference seemingly less
Than that between neighbourly hedges, depths of green.

Visions of a protestant

I saw a city paved with stretched-out people.
They were clothed but their feet, for safety's sake, were bare.
Toes nestled lightly in all colours of hair,
Fingers in fingers. It was a jigsaw puzzle
Solved in heart-pains, head-aches, watering eyes:
Death shrank to a speck high on a cliff of sighs.

I heard a city drowned in crystal thunder.
After a moment's silence, passionate saws
Were arguing chipboard into doors and windows.
A chalk-stick stumbled, broke itself in two.
Prices slashed, it screamed, *business as usual:*
The speck was a huge, cruel face. The crowd walked tall.

Cold Dawns

1. *Nightmare*

Busy as paddles in liquid, ratchets in clocks,
   An army is making new clouds above the Falls,
   And the rain-thin quilt we wear for rest unravels
And some are lulled, some trapped behind rattled locks.

And none can wake. Adrift in the bickering flow,
   That fills my kitchen with questions, still asleep,
   I pick up my kettle, turn, and almost leap
From the drawn blade flashed across the dawn-dark window.

2. *Maryville Avenue*

The frayed orange rug of a single lamp
Covers most of the street. Awake already,
The cement-works pants like a thirsty taxi.
The sky is one shade lighter than the tarmac,
But ghostly, still, in night-colour. Night-cold
Blooms in my doorway, solid with amazement.
The shiny, tidy dark of all I can see
Like the child's address – house-number to universe –
Or the confident water-rings of a thrown pebble,
Ends nowhere, has no end. How little the world is.
How it touches at every point, since your footsteps died across it.

Schoolgirl's Story

The news stayed good until Monday morning
When a taxi-driver was shot in the South of the city,
And his un-named schoolgirl-passenger injured.
Outside the window, clouds made changeable bruises
And spillings. Bad weather, taxi weather.
I picked up my dish, poured everything down the sink,
Unclogged it with bare fingers, ran for my coat,
Played back a dream of how it used to be,
Hearing about these things every day of the week
And not feeling cold and sick and hot: the beauty
    Of being nobody's lover.

I could hardly breath as I reached the school railings.
The clouds turned heavy again, opened fire
On my face and eyes with stinging rice-grains of hail.
Bad weather, taxi weather. *If it's not there*
I'll run, and my screams run with me, from here to Balmoral.
But the bike was on its stand in the shed as usual.
The square-root of the frame, graceful, ice-blue,
Cut me the old two ways: her nearness, her distance.
The sky paled. I began to look for her
Without seeming to. I stopped feeling sick for her.
    Another sickness took over.

Sunday Evening, Belfast 9

The family cars pour with a limousine swish
Down the sequestered avenue, their style
Not quite at ease, still conscious of arrival
And settlement in this almost solid parish.
Their careful drivers dipped as carefully to
The service, dropped the occasional autumn cough,
Then rose, shook hands, went fed and gilded through
A trace of mist, impatient to be off.
Under familiar trees at last, they bring
Magnified, watery shadows of good news
To driveways flooded with the shine of home,
And let the ritual die. A dog barks welcome.
The gravel settles down after applauding
their buoyant tyres, the highlights of their shoes.

Were their mild hopes alerted, for a mute
Second, as creed went naked on the street?
Walking the other side, I could have slipped
From any congregation save their own:
No stranger's guaranteed in a darkening town.
But I proved harmless, too. I read the pavement
And found the place where all the petals, blown
From yesterday's weddings, might have been translucent
Evidence of imaginary bushes,
Their everlasting roses specially bred
To shower a bride in delicate, soundless wishes.
I picked them out, like moonlight from stained glass,
Like glass from skin, waiting to cross the road,
Thinking: the gods will pass, the gods will pass.

The Lisburn Road List
(Variations on a Theme of Philip Larkin)

Glooms of old stone between shops,
And flat oases that blaze
All night, as ubiquitous
As copywriters' full-stops;
Churches and garages, both, in their different ways
Telling us this is a road going somewhere else:

And the buses to *Silverstream*
Via Shankhill, crowded as far
As the bone-hard, low-church seats
Punishing each rear,
And the dozens of other competitive notions of 'home',
And the eyes gazing carefully down on each 'somewhere else':

And the dusks, as mornful and slow
As the queue at the road-blocks,
A fire-engine screaming through,
Past the heavily-macintoshed barracks,
And the passers-by and the drivers thinking 'what's new?',
Thinking 'Jesus Christ, why don't I live somewhere else?'

And the gentler fantasies
For sale – a new colour-scheme,
Facials, cheap holidays,
And, if all else fails, an ice-cream;
And the intricate, well-worked hills undeceived by the dream
That life could be utterly different, somewhere else.

And at last the ephemeral I,
Observant or bored, but never
Doubting that summer will soon
Arrive to unveil a vast sky
Of rooftops and trees and the hard bright light of that question:
Where is your love for the life you had somewhere else?

Snowfire

The chimney-stacks had been variously feathered
As the north wind pushed across Maryville Avenue,
Whitening a corner here, a full side there,
And sometimes leaving the odd stack disregarded.
The roofs were white, the clouds a little less so.
They moved on fast, as if from the scene of a crime
They'd merely witnessed, but would be accused of.
At first, I thought it was only chimney-smoke
From a late-night hearth, trying to join the cloud-rush.
Then came a flashing, lit from beyond the apex.
Something on fire? It was bright enough, but silent:
A fire can't work without muttering, carelessly
Giving itself away. And now the wind
Was gushing up and up, and the roofs were dissolving,
And all the street was fainting and dazzling itself
In the fumey blast. I watched till my face went under,
The fire wanted in, and I had to shut the door.

Head Cold

River-mouth world, is it really a surprise
That a new tenant has judged your sinuses
An ideal home? Your breath aches through his coal-smoke
– Smell of the ancient tenderness of cities –
His fumey speeds sicken you like catarrh.

So many clouds, heroes of stone and shell
– The loveliest headache, if you could bear to look;
Every street laid with a different carpet,
Each garden its own mist of imagined spring,
Though a gloved thumb could wipe out any petal.

Strange city, doped and bright in your frosty vest,
Keep to your bed today, and fall in love
Again and again with the childhood illnesses
When your hands, unusually clean, turned the pages
Of adventures you could not possibly have.

Et Incarnatus Est

Windows are often loneliest when lighted,
Their silvery plenitude a kind of treason.
They smile, they seem to offer invitation
Between the last-leafed branches, but their eyes
Are kind only if you possess the keys.
Journeys towards such stars are best diverted.

Desire, though, being the senseless thing it is,
I know a certain window from all angles
And frequencies. The city's whole galère
Contains no poorer version of stained glass,
But it's among the daily miracles
When I check anxiously, find it still there,
Glass being so promiscuous with its spangles,
And light so frail, in cities such as this.

I'm happiest when it's invisible,
Sunk in the fireless black of the night sky,
A lovely emblem folded, put away,
And nothing left more innocent and hopeful
Than life itself. *There's no epiphany,*
No magic room: this is an empty house.
I can unthrone it, if I trust that blackness.

But when, through the burnt-out December trees,
The window shivers dreamily, plays at being
An earth-bound moon, then shows me, bright and full,
That soft shoulder-like curve, that frame of grace,
I breathe like a runner though I'm standing still.
I know what it is to have been a king
Once, and now to be frightened of a stable.

Some windows pierce the flesh but this, when lighted,
Is flesh itself, those fluids, sighs, word-world.
Other lights vanish or become blurred.
This burns the mind – not light, but living eyes,
Faultless, candid, where my last hope dies,
A child of hell, its death never completed.

Genius Loci

And through the blind glass that swings over every threshold
    I meet her eyes, touch her sleeve in an unfelt greeting,
And all the sad elms at their winter soliloquies, strive
    To copy her gestures, the grace of her clarification.
Each passage of footsteps insists on my terrified waiting
    Because she is all these opacities and rehearsals.

And in all the bright precincts we claimed, the ingenuous windows
    That gazed at the sky and saw nothing, are shocked into candour
Again as my hand cups a waterfall, studies a burning,
    Refining the one possibility, blatant, addicted,
And my lips brush a snow so unsettled and warm, with such lack
    Of demand, there is scarcely a trick of the air or the climate.

And if as I hurry home, rain-dazzled, down the long road
    With its blown-about pearls and its tapestry rucksack of hills,
She's there at the bus-stop, shivering, cloud-breathing, earthed,
    Waving an uncertain hand to attract my attention,
It's not in a wish to avoid her that I almost pass her;
    Simply, reality's never itself but a vision.

I have held her and lost her and lost her so questionably
    There isn't a stone unbereft nor unconsecrated.
All the hurrying cabs catch her up to some frangible safety:
    All the hedges weave gardens for her. She is every wind blowing,
Each darkness that's dressed in an impulse of light or water
    —An identity left, for a dying moment, wide open.

In Memory of a Friendship

Winter has reached the Spanish Steps, advancing
On tides of dirty suds like the landlady
Who mopped her way past literature, enticing
Tubercle bacilli from every mouse-hole.
The red street-carpets, swaggering muddily
Persuade the tourists to the Latin Quarter.
Hawkers, pipers, backpackers, gypsies, thieves,
Unabashed by the civic or the tonal,
Go on arguing as they've always done.
If someone's down to his last adjective,
Why should they care, among all these words and rain?

Joseph takes the day off for gardening.
He'd mentioned violets, and his friend forgot
The taste of coughed-up rust, fed on their sweetness.
The gifts seem lame, now, curiously weightless,
Loveletters to a sickbed, crushed unopened.
His own hand clenches, but he crowds the plot.
The buds twist on their necks to look at him,
Measure his skewed perspective, his unquickened
Muse. These were his painting-days. The rest
Is a double-grave, much visited, but modest,
The young men in it sharing, like two students,
Who think they've all their fame ahead of them.

Now sunlight soothes the convalescent steps
Where the tourists never leave, but simply swap
Countries, friends and occasionally, their jeans.
Epiphany's over, and the filthy carpets
Rolled and trucked away to be drycleaned.
The landlady mops the hall again, re-lets
The rooms to the one tenant who'll never leave.
The rooms learn to be quiet. But youth can't learn.
It takes offence at barely lived-in bones,
Watches, distraught, its ownerless name become
Less than the rain, less than the grave that drowns
Each spring, in earth-rich violets, acts of love.

How Can the Living Mourn Enough?

A car fled by with a shriek
And a wail. The trees fell down
And the dead were their thick green leaves

But the river that ran between us
Was the bright, dangerous one.

Heads hung between shoulder-blades
Like February flowers, intent
On the darkness at their feet

But the river that ran between us
was the bright, dangerous one.

Fingers pushed against eyes
Because tears let loose would become
Another universe
At the exit of our own

But the river that ran between us
Was the bright, dangerous one.

My fingers bunched cold cloth,
My lips were bruised by bone:
I wished to God I was dead.
The only loved are the dead.

But the river that ran between us
Was the bright, dangerous one.

Clouding the Borders
(View from a train window, Belfast-Dublin, March 1992)

The small hills glow their rain-deep green
In March as, in November, those
That hugged the sky round Iniskeen,
And fixed clay padlocks on our shoes.

Newry – where clouds already trust
Frail bodies to the most distant peaks.
North's westering gaze relaxes. Mist
And heather do their vanishing tricks.

No shadow of this landscape's mine:
No stick of it estranges me.
Kavanagh sowed his hills with coin.
We share the transient legacy.

I watch a ewe fold round her lamb,
Her brownish, and its snowy, fleece
Making in soft, unbroken form
The oldest word for *native place*.

The Release

When the plane lifts for the last time in the damp, grey, tender air
Over the small fields neatly swirled with mowing-furrows,
The Friesian cattle jumbled like dominoes
By their rusty out-house, I shall take one harsh breath
And fall instantly to dust, a thousand years old
Like the sybil freed from the curse that had kept her from dying.

Imperial Carbon
(for Franki Sewell)

       i love my sounds my sounds
       i love my sounds my sounds
       i love my
       i love my
           sounds sounds sounds sounds
         my my my my

West London nights, can I never stop coming back to you,
to your antediluvian plane trees, hanging on at the edge of the Green
where the still-companionable winos paddle the ring-pulls,
to your pavement-stash of papayas, red peppers, green peppers,
       plaintains
and your *English Pot's* peeping through curtains of coriander,
to your underpass charity-beds, your shop-doorway care-schemes,
where the one-to-one lesson is *spare us a bit of change of please?*
to the stains I don't want to explain, that will never wash out of
       the granite,
to your cop-cars stalled in the bottleneck, top-knots pulsating
but cool as a hand tapping time to the Kiss·FM cauldron

       i love my sounds my sounds
       i love my sounds my sounds
       i love my
       i love my
           sounds sounds sounds sounds
         my my my my

West London nights, I've been stuck in your skies for a century,
waiting for clearance, for mercy, rolling from sunset to sunset,
thinking I'd missed you in Marrakesh, burnt you in Belfast
but gravity turned out a winner. I'm yours, so don't watch me,
style-eyes appraising as if I'm a stranger. Don't bet on it, baby.
I'll just redistribute my weight a bit, look, now I'm moving
a treat to your beat, I'm native, I've family connections
among the neurotics of Acton, my Great-Auntie Mabel's
out pruning the roses or painting the railings, though really
the roses aren't hers, nor the railings – *Baby, the fifties are forty years*
       old now

            i love my sounds my sounds
            i love my sounds my sounds
            i love my
            i love my
                    sounds sounds sounds sounds
                my my my my

West London nights, if you want some identification,
the turbanned Muslim who keeps the off-licence knows me.
By the way, here's my key-of-the-door to my door of the day.
It leads to a well where the suicide speakers and systems
plunge in but keep swimming and scrabbling their way up the walls
– The Sultans of Ping, The Pogues, Petula, Deep Purple,
Vivaldi, Vysotsky – it leads to a holiday sadness
where I unpack those troubles, those overdue books and tall stories,
& my lungs ache after one night & no letters arrive & my typewriter
        always
needs the old kind of ribbon, a carbon, the buggers don't buy
        any more

            i love my sounds my sounds
            i love my sounds my sounds
            i love my
            i love my
                    sounds sounds sounds sounds
                my my my my

FROM **A STRANGE GIRL IN BRIGHT COLOURS**
(1973)

At Puberty

After rain
a blue light settled over the convent arches;

the naked asphalt astonished itself with diamonds;
even the washed-out plaster virgin
in the Bernadette Grotto, and the mulberry tree
propped up and barren of silk-worms,
stepped cleanly out of their decay.

From the back of the music lesson
a girl stared through a window
watching beam upon beam of realisation
incise the long mists of her childhood.

Her thirteenth spring
was born among the tattered pages
of the Older Children's Song Book.

Komme liebe Mai

sang the class, uneasily.
A new emotion,
innocent, classical,
yet making her shake and burn,
was softly unravelled
by the clear-eyed woman who sat
at the black Bosendorffer
with her coquettishness and her merciless
gentle arpeggios.

The elm-leaves turned, silver-backed,
on a wind coarse as hunger,

and nuns in their distant sanctuary,
the dark-blue brides of Christ,
closed their ears to the sin, the soft
tired alto of girls at puberty;
heard still a child's soprano.

O impossible miracles, light
out of straggle-rowed chairs
and school-room floor-boards

– the girl, pale as clouds,
stares for a year, aching
at the vision which has no need
of the speechless peasant,

which will suddenly vanish, leaving
only the deep river between them

– the woman who needed nothing,
and the child who promised everything.

The Inheritors

The street lights bronze the pale weatherboard
house-fronts. Beyond their heads, twelve bald
bulbs climb, one behind the other,
up Beech House, beechless as Buchenwald.

Plimsolls pound. A human shadow drops
and coils for cover behind the concrete stair.
The panda car is watching somewhere else.
The broken glass winks under the star.

Outside the fish-shop, knives are flashed.
Down in the play-park, five
girls curse and laugh and jounce the metal horse,
and wait all evening to be snatched alive.

These are the locks they'll wake behind, and these
hard sons the sort they'll struggle not to raise,
against the weatherboard and echoing stair,
down the cul-de-sacs as short as days.

FROM **UNPLAYED MUSIC**
(1981)

Unplayed Music

We stand apart in the crowd that slaps its filled glasses
on the green piano, quivering her shut heart.
The tavern, hung with bottles, winks and sways
like a little ship, smuggling its soul through darkness.
There is an arm flung jokily round my shoulders,
and clouds of words and smoke thicken between us.
I watch you watching me. All else is blindness.

Outside the long street glimmers pearl.
Our revellers' heat steams into the cold
as fresh snow, crisping and slithering
underfoot, witches us back to childhood.
Oh night of ice and Schnapps, moonshine and stars,
how lightly two of us have fallen in step
behind the crowd! The shadowy white landscape
gathers our few words into its secret.

All night in the small grey room
I'm listening for you, for the new music
waiting only to be played; all night I hear nothing
but wind over the snow, my own heart beating.

Death of Anna Pavlova

The swans are blue ice now. They remember nothing
– Katya, Marenka who snapped bread
out of my palm with spoon-cold beaks,
their eyes keen as copper. Another hand,
old and yellow-skinned, a tax-collector's,
strains from the bank's shade. I swim closer.
It knocks, knocks at my chest. Only stage fright!
Naiads bring rouged cotton, little swans
fuss at my ankles. I shall run alight
in my own white pool towards the crowds,
and show all Russia the wingspan of my love.

Listen, the applause breaks like gunfire
as bruised roses spin through the smoky shine
to drop at my feet. Real birds die like this,
heavily, their broken wings ungathered.
Even the mooning swans, necks dipped to blue
mirrors, die like this. But I laboured
each night until I held another truth.
Shoulders, elbows melted into sighs,
my hands were little flames, their ripples perming
to pure air, my long feet curved
like the beaks of magic birds that never touched
land or lake. In dying there's no art.
When blood carved the snow in the palace courtyard,
I heard theatres weep. The old dance,
choreographed in bones, is disappearing
between these sheets. I rasp my last cries
to prove them right, young soldiers, real swans
whose wings flashed treachery, who fished in silence.

A Marriage

Mondays, he trails burr-like fragments
of the weekend to London
– a bag of soft, yellow apples from his trees
– a sense of being loved and laundered.

He shows me a picture of marriage
as a small civilisation,
its parks, rosewood and broadloom;
its religion, the love of children

whose anger it survived
long ago, and who now return like lambs,
disarmed, adoring.
His wife sits by the window,

one hand planting tapestry daisies.
She smiles as he offers her the perfect apple.
On its polished, scented skin
falls a Renaissance gilding.

These two have kept their places,
trusting the old rules
of decorous counterpoint.
Now their lives are rich with echoes.

Tomorrow, she'll carry a boxful
of apples to school. Her six year olds
will weigh, then eat them, thrilling
to a flavour sharp as tears.

I listen while he tells me about her sewing,
as if I were the square of dull cloth
and his voice the leaping needle
chasing its tail in a dazzle of wonderment.

He places an apple in my hand;
then, for a moment, I must become his child.
To look at him as a woman
would turn me cold with shame.

The Skin Politic

Sails for the dark blue trade routes
Guns for the jungle
Mulberry trees for Brick Lane
White skins for England.

Smiles for a passport
Pavements for wet walking
Ramadan for emptiness
White skins for England.

Airmail for memories
Shudders for dark nights
Swastikas for bus shelters
White skins for England.

Long words for governments
Short words for street corners
Last rites for promises
White skins for England.

In Pear Tree Road

Only plane trees stood
Now in Pear Tree Road.
My father mourned white orchards,
But I was glad,

Especially in autumn
When the wind laid tiles
Of their broad, delicate leaves
To colour the stone miles.

I kicked them high and wide;
Pleased with the patterns, took
A rustling quire of them
To page my heaviest book.

Many were merely brown,
Some still green as May.
The best had put on all
Their rich seasons to die,

Hanging tight until
That final crimsoning
When the small sun had pressed
A flame hand to each skin.

Rules for Beginners

They said: 'Honour thy father and thy mother.
Don't spend every evening at the Disco.
Listen to your teachers, take an O level
or two. Of course, one day you'll have children.
We've tried our best to make everything nice.
Now it's up to you to be an adult!'

She went to all the 'X' films like an adult.
Sometimes she hung around the Mecca Disco.
Most of the boys she met were dead O level,
smoking and swearing, really great big children.
She had a lot of hassle with her mother;
it was always her clothes or her friends that weren't nice.

At school some of the teachers were quite nice,
but most of them thought they were minding children.
'Now Susan,' they would say, 'You're nearly adult
– behave like one!' The snobs taking O level
never had fun, never went to the Disco;
they did their homework during 'Listen with Mother'.

She said: 'I'd hate to end up like my mother,
but there's this lovely bloke down at the Disco
who makes me feel a lot more like an adult.'
He murmured – 'When I look at you, it's nice
all over! Can't you cut that old O level
scene? Christ, I could give you twenty children!'

He had to marry her. There were three children
– all girls. Sometimes she took them to her mother
to get a break. She tried to keep them nice.
It was dull all day with kids, the only adult.
She wished they'd told you that, instead of O level.
Sometimes she dragged her husband to the Disco.

She got a part-time job at the Disco,
behind the bar; a neighbour had the children.
Now she knew all about being an adult
and honestly it wasn't very nice.
Her husband grumbled – 'Where's the dinner, mother?'
'I'm going down the night-school for an O level,

I am,' said mother. 'Have fun at the Disco,
kids! When you're an adult, life's all O level.
Stay clear of children, keep your figures nice!'

Before These Wars

In the early days of marriage
my parents go swimming in an empty sea
– cold as an echo, but somehow *theirs*,
for all its restless size.

From the year 1980 I watch them
putting on the foaming lace.
The sun's gold oils slide from their young skin
and hair as they surface

to fling each other handfuls
of confetti – iced tinsel
and tissue, miniature horseshoes
of silver, white poppy petals.

I search their laughter in vain:
no baby twinkles there,
and Hitler has not yet marched on Poland
beyond the cornflower waves

this print shows pewter.
But that the possible happens
eventually, everyone knows...
and when they swim away

the unsettled water fills
with shuddery, dismantled weddings,
a cloud unfurled like an oak tree,
time twisting as it burns.

The Girl in the Cathedral
(for Andrew and Joanna)

Daring to watch over Martyrs and Archbishops
Stretched in their full-length slumbers, sharp-nosed Deans,
Princes and Knights still dressed for wars as dim
As bronze, slim feet at rest upon the flanks
Of long-unwhistled hounds; daring the chills
And dusts that cling to stiffly soaring branches,
This small eloquence is a stone so plain
It cannot go unread, a chiselled spray
Of drooping buds, a name, a date, an age.
Susannah Starr died at ten years old,
And no one knows why her timid presence
Should be commended here. While history filled
The log-books of these lives, she sat apart,
A well-bred child, perhaps, patient with tutors
And needlepoint, perhaps a foundling, saved
By some lean churchman, warming to his duty.
Quietly during 1804
The blind was drawn, the half-stitched sampler folded.
Whoever mourned her must have carried weight
And bought her this pale space to ease his grief
As if such sainted company could speed
Her journeying soul, or because he guessed
The power of one short name and 'ten years old'
To strip the clothes from all these emperors,
And rouse her simple ghost, our pointless tears.

Almost in Walking Distance

Two centuries ago they would have taken
this same short cut through the farm,
the rough, scrubbed boys and girls to whom
corn-fields were work-a-day. In tight best boots
for the Sabbath, laughing tumbled country vowels,

on mornings blue and full of bells as this one,
they would have skirted the plait-haired rows
all the way to the crumbly lanes of Chaldon
and the parish church, their star,
cradled in a cluster of bent yews.

What's altered in the scene
isn't just the split sack of pesticide, blowing
from a hedge, the tractor waiting on the hill,
or the bare sting of my legs against the stalks;
it is my aimless pleasure in the walk
and the edge of melancholy it lends the bells
calling me to a hope I cannot enter
across fields I know well, yet do not know.

Three Poets Play the Saké Cup Game

A print dating from the Edo period shows a group of Japanese poets
floating saké cups on a stream. One poet would launch the cup,
and another, standing at a certain distance downstream, try to compose
a haiku by the time the cup reached him. In the print, the resulting
poems are being hung to dry on the branches of a tree.

1

Tying his proud syllables
to a scented branch,
the poet hears laughter.
He turns and sees the cup
lodged winking in some reeds.
It will never pass him now.
As life begins, the poet muses,
so it stops, without warning.
Haiku is the game in the middle.
'Have I won?' he asks. 'Or lost?'

2

The orange saké cup
throbs on the bright stream
with petals, like a migraine.
It's only one word he wants,
one last, ripe cherry
brimming with the juice of his poem.
The cup weaves nearer. Demons
toss him a flashy adjective.
He sighs, and scribbles.
Sometimes he can't bear to be a poet.

3

The idea grows.
He must be careful, careful.
Never mind the jeering,
winter's a difficult season
and this could be its soul.
He mustn't let it slip by
as the saké cup slips by.
When he wakes from the poem,
it's dark, the cherry has dropped
many leaves, his friends have gone.

FROM **STAR WHISPER**
(1983)

Star Whisper
(for Eugene Dubnov)

If you dare breathe out in Verkhoyansk
You'll get the sound of life turning to frost
As if it were an untuned radio,
    A storm of dust.

It's what the stars confess when all is silence
– Not to the telescopes, but to the snow.
It hangs upon the trees like silver berries
    – Iced human dew.

Imagine how the throat gets thick with it,
How many *versts* there are until the spring,
How close the blood is, just behind the lips
    And tongue, to freezing.

Here, you can breathe a hundred times a minute,
And from the temperate air still fail to draw
Conclusions about whether you're alive
    – If so, what for.

Writing the City

Rhymes, like two different hands joining,
are those slightly archaic correspondences
I look for when in trouble. It's so easy
to start panicking in cities.

All roads lead to each other, sharing slick
anecdotes of combustion. They sell
tin lollipops, barren islands
and the one-way look for city faces.

Things happen and unhappen; cars, like eyelids,
blink time away. I'm due for demolition...
That's why I stand so long in the Poetry Section,
and buy apples just to slice them into cradles.

A Case of Deprivation

A shelf of books, a little meat
– How rich we felt, how deeply fed –
But these are not what children eat.

The registrar rose from his seat.
Confetti danced, and thus were wed
A shelf of books, a little meat.

We sang, for songs are cheap and sweet.
I he state dropped by with crusts of bread
But these are not what children eat.

They came, demanding trick or treat.
We shut our eyes and served instead
A shelf of books, a little meat.

Then on our hearts the whole world beat,
And of our hopes the whole world said
But these are not what children eat.

Two shadows shiver on our street.
They have a roof, a fire, a bed,
A shelf of books, a little meat
– But these are not what children eat.

Lullaby for a First Child

This timid gift I nurse
as the one clear thing I can do.
I am new and history-less
as the name on your wrist, as you.
But flesh has stored a deep kindness
ready to welcome you.
Take it, a little silver
into your small purse.
There it will gather interest
– the warm, bright weight of you.

Skins

There are those that time will carelessly perfect:
Leather, wood and brick fall derelict
As if aware they charmed us as they slip;
This deal table, strung like a harp
With a silky glissando of dark grain
Blooms like a lover from the hands it's known.
Scrawlings of knife and bottle, child and guest
Have warmed its heart, a rough autumnal feast
Spilled into soil, becoming nutriment;
The wood's more deeply wood because of it.
But there are others, the most loved and rare,
Time told them once, of which the years despair.
Laughter has scribbled not itself but pain.
Each face is fallen on hard times of bone.
Money will court them first, and then deride them.
There are no masks but sorry stones to hide them.
Yet to the end they haunt disgusted mirrors,
As close as love, and steal with snow-lipped fingers
From little, lying, scented jars each night,
Skins that are pillow-shadows by first light.

March, Happy Valley

Days that are finely stretched and luminous
as the paper of a Chinese lantern, keep
the birds up late and whispering across
the valley, where a massive wind feigns sleep.
All down the heath-side, dangerously close
as heart-beats to a foot that wades deep grass,
hang violets in the strangeness of their blue.
Luggageless, perennially new,
with ancient heads that they can only bend,
they have arrived more quietly than the dew
to feel the perfect cold of where they stand.

The country has a used, dishonest face,
a look of sour back-streets where trade has died
though half the windows still pretend with lace.
Spring, the sweet spring, is a refugee child
grown old before his time, a hope displaced.

Museum

Pro bono publico,
bright wood, clear labels;
a tasteful history
of sand and fossils,

motto-bearing plates
and, along one wall,
like the Apocalypse,
'The Coal Coast' in oils.

Out on the concrete copy,
dogs are walked. The flat
water takes a slice
of sun from the smokeless sky.

The schools line up to go,
but the men in caps
linger shadowily
over toy-town mines, dolls' ships.

They get the place by heart
like the last day at the pit
or the drawer in the kitchen
where the strainer's kept.

Cherchez l'ail

London that night was held by golden ropes
    Fraying through the river's black.
The 'Queen of Spain' with all her costly lives
Sat tight, as we sat, formal in our hopes,
The bottle on its ice-bed leaning back.
We touched the cloth with bright, impatient knives.

Tides turn, the damaged love-boat drifts away;
    The marriage-teasers walk
The plank, and one in torment almost screams,
But smiles instead. I sniffed my hands next day
To light those flames that stroked our ice-chink talk,
To meet you on the garlic breath of dreams.

Siren

Your children are your innocence, you prize them
greedily, three pink fingers dipped in honey.
At night, three souls slide in their perfect skins
into a rippling length of light. You bend,
damp-curled, still marvelling at the little bud
of abandonment, each tiny, cracked omphalos,
how it is almost an opening that you
might slip into, ticklish, precipitous,
a hair's breadth widening from tenderness
to pain. Sleeked as if by recent birth,
hair cleaves to each small skull, neat as your hand
to well-soaped limbs. So you relinquish power
to babble and disport with the loopy tongues
of child-talk. You have three faces now
with three clean smiles for the mother goddess.
I stand apart, waving a small goodbye,
and noticing that my innocence too has drifted
off with your limpid fleet, just out of reach,
leaving me pure sex, a dangerous pulsing,
a light that sings and warns on the bare ledge of self.

The Hebrew Class

Dark night of the year, the clinging ice
a blue pavement-Dresden,
smoking still, and in lands more deeply frozen,
the savage thaw of tanks:

but in the Hebrew class it is warm as childhood.
It is Cheder and Sunday School.
It is the golden honey of approval,
the slow, grainy tear saved for the bread

of a child newly broken
on the barbs of his Aleph-Bet,
to show him that knowledge is sweet
– and obedience, by the same token.

So we taste power and pleasing,
and the white wand of chalk lisps on the board,
milky as our first words.
We try to shine for our leader.

How almost perfectly human
this little circle of bright heads bowed before
the declaration of grammatical law.
Who could divide our nation

of study? Not even God.
We are blank pages hungry for the pen.
We are ploughed fields, soft and ripe for planting.
What music rises and falls as we softly read.

Oh smiling children, dangerously gifted ones,
take care that you learn to ask why,
for the room you are in is also history.
Consider your sweet compliance

in the light of that day when the book
is torn from your hand;
when, to answer correctly the teacher's command,
you must speak for this ice, this dark.

An Easter Garland

1

The flowers did not seem to unfurl from slow bulbs.
They were suddenly there,
shivering swimmers on the edge of a gala
– nude whites and yellows shocking the raw air.

They'd switched themselves on like streetlamps
waking at dawn, feeling wrong,
to blaze nervously all day at the chalky sky.
Are they masks, the frills on bruised babies?
I can't believe in them,
as I can't believe in the spruces and lawns and bricks
they publicise, the misted light of front lounges
twinned all the way down the road,
twinned like their occupants, little weather-house people
who hide inside and do not show their tears
– the moisture that drives one sadly to a doorway.

2

My father explained the workings of the weather-house
as if he seriously loved such things,
told me why Grandpa kept a blackening tress
of seaweed in the hall.
He was an expert on atmosphere,
having known a weight of dampness
– the fog in a sick brother's lungs
where he lost his childhood; later, the soft squalls
of marriage and the wordier silences.

In the atmosphere of the fire
that took him back to bone
and beyond bone, he smiled.
The cellophaned flowers outside
went a slower way, their sweat
dappling the linings of their glassy hoods.

3

My orphaned grass
is standing on tiptoe to look for you.
Your last gift to a work-shy daughter
was to play out and regather
the slow thread of your breath

behind the rattling blades,
crossing always to darker green,
till the lawn was a well-washed quilt
drying, the palest on the line,
and you rested over the handlebars
like a schoolboy, freewheeling
through your decades of green-scented, blue,
suburban English twilights.

4

In the lonely garden of the page,
something has happened to your silence.
The stone cloud has rolled off.
You make yourself known
as innocently abrupt
as the flared wings of the almond,
cherry, magnolia;
and I, though stupid with regret,
would not be far wrong
if I took you for the gardener.

The Emigrée

There was once a country... I left it as a child
but my memory of it is sunlight-clear
for it seems I never saw it in that November
which, I am told, comes to the mildest city.
The worst news I receive of it cannot break
my original view, the bright, filled paperweight.
It may be at war, it may be sick with tyrants,
but I am branded by an impression of sunlight.

The white streets of that city, the graceful slopes
glow even clearer as time rolls its tanks
and the frontiers rise between us, close like waves.
That child's vocabulary I carried here
like a hollow doll, opens and spills a grammar.
Soon I shall have every coloured molecule of it.
It may by now be a lie, banned by the state
but I can't get it off my tongue. It tastes of sunlight.

I have no passport, there's no way back at all
but my city comes to me in its own white plane.
It lies down in front of me, docile as paper;
I comb its hair and love its shining eyes.
My city takes me dancing through the city
of walls. They accuse me of absence, they circle me.
They accuse me of being dark in their free city.
My city hides behind me. They mutter death,
and my shadow falls as evidence of sunlight.

The Most Difficult Door

There is an ageing mirror by the stairs
And, next to that, the most difficult of doors.
This is where we live, the home's true heart.
Its furnishings, heaped for some moonlight flit,
Are combs and hats and scarves in slip-knots, all
Embodying the female principle!

I sometimes think they must have swum like clouds,
My daughters, through those sea-blue altitudes
Of birth, where I was nothing but the dark
Muscle of time. I bear the water-mark
As proof, but that my flesh could be so filled
And concentrated, heart to heart with child

– It mystifies me now. I want to draw
One back, and this time feel a proper awe
For the tiny floater, thumb-sucking on its rope,
Slumbering in the roar of the mother-ship,
Or let my palm ride switchback on the billows
Kicked in my skin by silvery, unborn heels.

Instead, through thinnest glass I watch them drift
At leisure down their self-sufficient street;
Their territory might be the whole of time
Like that of lovers in some midnight game,
This house their port where indolently they sight
Far out at sea the changing play of light.

Sea restlessness! It haunts the oldest vessel
– A shanty murmuring under a torn sail
That no harbour is safe, nor should be safe.
Only deep waters lend full weight to life.
The maths of stars is learned by navigation,
And the home's sweetness by the salty ocean.

This glass could cut a vista down the years,
Gathering suburban satins and veneers
To a sleepy London bedroom. Hair, long-greyed,
Glows animal again. They're half afraid
To see themselves, so shiny, crimped and pressed
– My grandparents, doll-perfect, wedding-dressed.

And now its stare borrows an older face
– My own. The moon inimitably displays
Her sun-love. Through these veils we snatch from death
Our dusty matter, light its eyes with myth.
Nature wants Children. Children sometimes want
The moon, the cup, the shield, the monument.

We've watched the comb reap sparks from our live hair;
Now for the putting-on of mock despair
As timeless as these little pouts and twists
– A rite we go through as the cold glass mists.
We know the brightness in each painted eye
Must often be the brightness of goodbye.

My floating daughters, as I leave I'll see
How you will one day look as you leave me,
How touch draws back, malingering, though the breeze
Of night is tugging gently at our sleeves.
Be wary, but don't fear the darkening street.
I give you this, my opened map of flight.

Heart Sufferer

He stands in his kingdom of cloth, the long rolls
heaped in a stifling rococo all around him,
and smiles at the visitors' compliments. His eyes
are calm, however. He is no emperor now,
merely a guide. Business is a small thing
compared to a Bach fugue or even a prelude,
though balancing by day his lost currencies.

He speaks his adopted tongue with a fluent crafting,
except for a few cut vowels. But the poets he quotes
are all Hungarian, all untranslated.
He is recomposing a suite of piano music
remembered across the noise of thirty years,
this businessman who makes out an order so briskly
– three metres of small-check gingham in muted green.

His customers tonight are an English couple.
The man beats him occasionally at chess.
The woman he doesn't know. The cloth is a gift.
She presses it to her face, smelling the sweetness
of an orange giving its gold to the treacherous north.
He waits upon her choice, feeling December
creep from the walls, whisper up through his soles.

Here are satiny linings, cerulean
glints from the rarest birds, the earliest summers.
Here are the stripes of crops, a snow of flowers;
and now the flattened cities, tanks, collapsed
angles of aircraft; table-cloths once dappled
by the Sabbath candles, ravelling up in flame;
small bodies sewn into the colourless dresses.

He turns off the lights (no one else is allowed to,
he explains shyly – it's an old superstition)
and thinks of his tall sons, how they will never
wake the switches of his dying kingdom.
He climbs the stairs slowly, examining
the coats of his two visitors – brash young cloth,
not lasting. His heart warns him, beat by beat.

With luck, he'll leave its music at the door
of his favourite cellar bar. A dish of prawns
is light, easily swallowed. He breaks the necks
deftly, sucks the juice from each stalked head,
and wonders at his sin, the sea-clean flavour.
At pavement-level, London chains its gods
in light; he worships none, but wins each day
by his own kind of fasting and atonement,
time become paper-thin as the map of prawn shells.

Geography Lesson

Here we have the sea of children; here
A tiny piece of Europe with dark hair.
She's crying. I am sitting next to her.

Thirty yellow suns blobbed on cheap paper,
Thirty skies blue as a Smith's Salt-wrapper
Are fading in the darkness of this weeper.

She's Czechoslovakia. And all the desks
Are shaking now. The classroom window cracks
And melts. I've caught her sobs like chicken-pox.

Czechoslovakia, though I've never seen
Your cities, I have somehow touched your skin.
You're all the hurt geography I own.

Phaedrus

The souls of lovers, said Socrates
to his young companion,

can complete their wings only
by embracing Philosophy.

The way hard, these friends
paddled the stream, arousing

a bright complication of water.
Through the hot midday

their silvery dialectic
shimmered below plane-leaves.

Summer wings stirring the air,
love talked itself to oblivion.

They parted not with a kiss
but a prayer, honouring wisdom.

Double Exposure
(for David Rumens)

Come into my room now your better half
has floated off from you a little; don't
mock, don't make a noise, don't spill the coffee.
I'm playing house here, but it's tree-top-frail,
so leave your gales and lightnings at the door
and come and give me your blessing – what else
are the latest-model modern husbands for?

You could play, too. Why not become a student
chemist, crash out on the sisal floor
of an obscure first-year philosopher?
Show her some snaps – not of your holidays
or chess triumphs, but the future – two giant babies
who come alive and roam about the room,
eating cake and groaning as you kiss her?
The bed looks comfy, but won't give you shelter.
You'll have to pick a quieter afternoon
to marvel at the virgin you'd uncover
– double-exposed with baby-scrawls of silver.

Here, where our past and present planes bisect,
it seems quite natural, after dark, to find
the window holds a city and a room,
exchanging surfaces on blue-black film.
Look how the Post Office Tower wears my wardrobe.
A train, hurrying out of Euston, glides
its amber wishes through me every night,
until I pinch the curtains close, decide
it's time for old techniques of black on white.

Above the single bed I've tacked a 'Klimt'.
It's called *Fulfilment*. If you'd noticed it,
you might have found it raised a few light questions.
A joke, as bitter as its after-taste?
A profound statement on the spiritual
rewards of celibacy? A sly confession
or just a wish, perhaps? You might have seen
more intersections than at Clapham Junction,
had you looked up, and traced
the flow of gilded dressing-gowns, their scrolls
converging on a decadent embrace.

'Time will say nothing but I told you so'
– Is that our rubric? Janis, ten years dead,
still howls her living anger through my head.
'Freedom's just another word for nothing
left to lose.' What can an expert say –
that freedom's not like being sent a cheque,
nor working after midnight on a high,
nor walking miles, just for the hell of it?

That mine, at least, brims with the luxury
we thought we didn't have, and every lack.
An unmade past is like an unmade bed
at three a.m. Since you arrived, these walls
haven't stopped flickering with the lantern-show,
Fulfilment, all its tricks and vérité.

On a night that's Mediterranean-warm and dusty,
we drift to where the space-invaders flash,
and street-wise reflexes are newly honed
by the imminent loss of ready cash.
The Camden of stripped pine and harebell-shades
on bent, brass stems, has locked itself away
for dinner, *en famille*. Greek music braids
a brightened, scabby tenement, marked For Sale.
The plum-haired sons and daughters of tavernas
gesture like figures on an ancient frieze
though words and clothes declare them Londoners.

I leave you video-gazing, leave you winning.
Small faces lift for kisses, nonchalant.
I'm clumsy at this *weekend-parenting*
but no one cries or argues. Back indoors,
I add another bookshelf (just a brick
at each end, and a plank across) and stack
the comics and Sunday papers that you've left
and that I'll never read – one more sad sifting
of true from new. And then it's time for bed
– earlier than I'd planned, since, in the dark
it's harder to see double, hard to see
a thing, in fact. Freedom's just floorboards, walls,
a bit of glass. And yet it felt like home
till you arrived and showed me where I am.

FROM **DIRECT DIALLING**
(1985)

Pavane for the Lost Children

When you rest in my arms and your heart
quietens against mine
I think of a midnight kitchen,
the kettle muttering on the lowest gas,
and the baby forgetting to feed,
lips plumped like a little mollusc
that is almost losing its grip.
They could not relinquish survival,
those lips; I knew what they dreamed of
would keep arousing them
to fits of greedy, absent-minded tugging.
So I sat on, enthralled
by thirst, by plenitude.

This, too, is our grown-up devotion
when fatigue is most pressing:
to pretend we will never put each other down
and drift singly away on
sleep's disappointing persuasions;
such lowly forms of life, so deeply marine,
we cannot move apart, or know what time is,
but are turned like bivalves on the lifting wave
that has promised us to the sand.

Time Trouble

I know all about these German wrist-watches.
They try to wake you with tinny, insect-like tunes
as the digits flip over on your bedside table
and my old-fashioned minute-hand
flies to your neck and whispers nervously
with that little pad of fat where your head is thrown back
because you're still in an ecstasy of sleep,
and your suitcase not yet packed.

Once upon a time
they'd take me to admire the German clock
in the museum. There were wooden figures inside it:
Jesus at wooden supper
with his twelve wooden apostles.
And when it struck three, they said,
the apostles filed out
and all bowed woodenly to Jesus
except Judas, who swung round the wrong way.

I never stayed to see this remarkable dumb-show.
By a minute to three, I was going to be sick;
I turned my back on the clock, the crowd
fell apart with a hiss.
As I race down the shadowless aisles,
though the horrible whirring has not yet begun,
I can see it all perfectly
– mad Jesus, his nodding guests,
and Judas, the simple materialist,
turning on his clockwork,
showing us his chalk-white face.

Vocation

Is it poetry I'm after at those moments when
I must clothe your hands in mine or comfort your shoulders
– so bare and neglected sometimes when we wake –
or press your mouth to taste its uncurling flower?
Is that which seems so fleshly and truthful merely
a twisted track into words, a way to leave you
for your image? Art is tempting, a colourful
infidelity with the self, and doubly feigning
when what is repossessed secretly by one
was made by two. And I wish I could pour a poetry-vodka
into twin glasses we'd gulp unanimously
('I poison myself for your health' the appropriate toast)
but only a poet would have acquired the taste
for such a strange distillation; you'd never warm

to heavy-petting dactyls, the squeak and creak
from locked, suburban stanzas. And so my fingers,
dancing alone, are less than content. They perceive
how they have clung to moral adolescence.
Their vocation now could be simply to talk to your skin,
to take you at kissing-time; later, to close your eyes
by stroking the lashes lightly over cheekbones
flushed with some high, bright, childish fever, and so
write the poem in the touch-shapes of darkness
and let it end there...They are on the tip of trusting
this silent, greyish room, its astonishing view
fading from metaphor to the life with you.

Revolutionary Women

Nechayev, dreaming of Tsar-death,
wrote about three categories of women,
and how they could be harnessed to the cause.
The first he dismissed as painted, empty.
You could twist them, break them, toss them away.
The second were good comrades, passionate
idealists, willing workers,
but dangerous finally, and disappointing
– their values weren't political at all:
they too must be discarded or reformed.
The third kind were the true revolutionaries;
deft with gun-oil, bullets, high explosive.
They'd take a lover only for his secrets,
milk him fast and leave him in his blood.

I know I'm with the second sort, cherishing
nothing better than a just cause,
except perhaps the man who'd die for it;
who grows entranced, watching allegiance crumble
and rebuild itself in curious gothic snow
like candles at the hovering hour of sleep.

Turning soup into a bowl I've started
at a white face in the china, both yours,
Nechayev, and that of any bourgeois
gazing up in naked appetite.
This is what causes the strong hand to falter.
Armies, official and unofficial, learn
that what they kill aren't men, or are only men.
But we, that regiment of the starry-eyed
you need and fear and try to educate,
who type your manifestoes through the night,
may still in the morning be discovered,
the counter-revolution breathing gently
beside us on the pillow, while the Tsar
goes to breakfast, and his men to torture.
In our loose night-gowns warm and obvious,
too slippery to cement a single brick
of the just state, even the state of marriage
– Nechayev, you'd be right to gun us down.

In the Cloud of Unknowing

Goodbye, bright creature.
I would have had you
somewhere on solid earth,
wings clipped to pale

shoulder-blades,
and your fleecy head
a chrysanthemum, darkly
grown from my pillow.

I would have kept my tongue
for what salt weepings
it could tease from your finest
silences.

But it was written
into your book of life
that I should be brief.
Forbidden to count

the ways, denied
et cetera,
I worshipped the stone
from your supper-time plum,

the little hairs gleaned
in tears from the sheet.
Metaphysical desire
was all they would bear,

a bandage of art
for the low sob
of the vernacular,
a condition of prayer.

Now when I wake
and the dawn light names
your perfect absence,
I am at home,

lapped again
in my earliest language,
the vocatives tense
with desire and distance:

'Thou who art called
the Paraclete';
'After this our exile';
'Oh Sacred Heart!'

Dear iconoclast
forgive these texts
their cloudy haloes.
The intent pen burns

its slow path through
the slant rain of Greek,
the stars of Hebrew
...to touch your hem?

No, it was never
possible.
The old mystics knew
as they closed the book

on the dancing colours,
worn out with words
never made flesh
and with flesh that fought

their long abstraction.
They listened a moment;
the breath-soft foot-step
in the cloisters faded

as always to sighs;
the cold congress of leaves
in darkening autumn;
the wind's dissolution.

Outside Oswiecim

1

Let me tell you the story of days, handsomely printed
in dawn and darkness, in sleep
and in burnt-eyed longing for sleep.

2

It puzzles the secular light, this polyphony
of dim cries. I wasn't there, I heard nothing,
but the air fills, and my breath can only sing them.

3

When the train banged to a stop and whispered 'where?',
then they began. Some rose, some fell. *The sky
rushed in like sea, we opened our mouths, it drank us.*

4

The hardest hope to lose is the last and smallest.
Those words on the gate, some dreamed of them, and loved
to walk in their shade, suck out the iron of their promise.

5

In the night, the light; in the light, the wire;
in the wire, the heart; in the heart, the world;
in the world, Oswiecim.

6

Dumb narrative curiosity keeps you from the wire
how many times? You watch yourself, amazed,
whipped to a panting run past outstretched arms.

7

It was Erev Shabbat, evil was fallible.
A shaved girl smiled in the sun. An angel had murmured
'Amen' before he saw the gesturing dead.

8

And what if his lord had heard that some of them
were raging animals, and still sent daybreak, still
sent no one to stroke them with their names?

9

No, no, the question is obsolete.
Nothing sees nothing. Mercy was up to us.
Our mouths bit down on nothing.

10

Emblem, exhibit, witness – Husserl's suitcase
flanked the rust-brown pile. The cold twine of its handle
I touch, then grasp for a faceless, weightless stanza.

11

Child, enchanted at gun-point, whose child are you?
Come here, take off your cap, don't cry.
How is it possible I can make no difference?

12

Oh they crowd in, death's kindergarten. Small grazes
scared them once. Their eyes are always yours.
I'd take their pain, here, where your absence is.

13

I loved in you, yes, what made you strangest.
The desert gave you its shadows. I'd watch for ever
the poise of your smile, its mocking tenderness.

14

Another race is only an other, strolling
on the far side of our skin, badged with his weather.
In love or hate we cast looks, hooks; get it wrong.

15

How shall I bear your indifference without hate?
It stirs in the dust, a length of hose. If I burn
how shall I not flex my whip near your eyes?

16

No, come away, bury yourself in the pit
of tears, be ash and stone, your stare
like his, a star.

17

They beckoned, they turned their limbs this way and that,
they whispered, you tried to get near enough to hear,
but the heat roared at you – *take your eyes, run.*

18

Not 'the six million', not 'the holocaust',
not words that mass-produce, but names. One name;
Husserl's, perhaps. His favourite food, his new watch.

19

Chosen to illustrate the Shibboleth's Tale;
An illumination from the Book of Fire,
Sand and Next Year; chosen to be most mortal,

Our pyramid swam and sank through the nitrogen
Fog as starving crystals ate our air.
Christ, to whom the soldier said 'Go on,

Call down your god if he's got ears and brains',
You would have understood our short-breathed terror.
Poor rebel son, you shared our tribal chains
That day, but now we wipe you from our mirror.

So we died for the last unforgeable scrap
– Our land. Got free for being something harder
Than walking zoo-meat. Fought like the Crusader
To nail our resurrection to the map.

A Prague Dusk, August 21st 1983

About a subjugated plain,
Among its desperate and slain,
The Ogre stalks with hands on hips,
While drivel gushes from his lips.
                    W.H. AUDEN

1

When his broad shoulders turn
in their leaf-coloured uniform
and square up to a doorway
on Revolucni Street,
he might be any soldier
and the bar, any girl,
its response no more than a certain
heightened inattention.
He orders beer and seems
as innocent as his thirst,
straining his young white throat
to greet the last drop,
but the pearl of Mitteleuropa
has dimmed behind him;
shadows slide unchecked
from the medallioned buildings
scaffolded up to the waist,
numb veterans who have learned
how short the life of honour.

He smiles, provincial, brash,
half-tame. The careful hands
that have served his purposes
slink off and busy themselves
with rows of glasses, small
change. Eyes follow him out,
each glint of hate a coin
with its own private value.

2

That he could not master speech
no longer seems important.
Perhaps only a poet
word-trafficking in the free-
market economy
of Oxford or New York
would have thought it a fatal weakness.
One blast of his breath was enough
to seal the twelve bridges.
With a few phrasebook phrases
he is armed for years to surprise
and amuse the populace,
his weight sunk in its silence.
Impassioned flattery
on the cut of his Westerner jeans
is not expected when,
naked as his fists,
he strides down Vaclavski Namesti
with his shuffling train of echoes:
what happens, happens without us.
We forget only the present.
It is the glue of memory
that seals, like morphine, the nerves
of the empty August city.

3

Going home on the metro
the children chatter
but the mother is almost asleep.
Some sweet, unscripted dream
wanders across her face,

follows the droop of her arm
to the grasses that nod in her lap.
It's already dark
on the staircase where she hushes
and stumbles; light from outside
shines on the two pairs of shoes
placed at each nuptial doorway,
intimate and exhausted,
moored like little boats
in an ocean of drudgery.
When she too, at last,
is sitting in stockinged feet
and the children asleep,
she will recall each detail
of the picnic: how the country
they walked through never changed,
monotonous and tender
as the afternoons of motherhood;
how tall the grass became
when they lay down to rest
and the stalks rose silvery miles
and whispered to the sky.

Blockade

Europe has been broken:
a panacea of banks,
steel cladding, the black
fugue of Berlin.

Oh Linden Tree, oh Linden
I cannot breathe
without your small hands, your great shade.

ICONS, WAVES
(1986)

Icons, Waves

The scalding gulp that almost clears the glass,
love rushes to the human eye, and lends it
illusions of a focus so exact,
a driver might lurch out, steer straight to death.
But we, late diners who've got tired of dining
and turned to iconography, believe
inaccuracy is also revelation.
Under the broad lamp with its singing bulb,
we stare into each other's brightest stares,
unselfed with curiosity, archaic,
and paint each other in a universe
where nothing's lost by lying in perspective:
I have the details – red formica table,
rinsed baked bean tin with its clutch of spoons,
your flatmate's skinny plant, the sallow glitter
of our once quickly filled and emptied glasses.

*

It was a dangerous ship we put to sea in;
over-freighted, dressed in Baltic ice,
crewed by the breath-clouds that had been your story.
Burning hope like kerosene, it suffered
the magnets of exile, every wave.
And though we raised our glasses, splashed our beer
with the sly diminutive brewed for thirty degrees
of ideology and new-year frost,
our toast was the old harbour of Atlantis.
I'd come aboard for word-trade, narrative,
warm money in my hand. You silenced me,
and it was then I felt the monster turn
his armoured intricacies under the waves,
and follow us like whispers, like ice.

*

So we'll be ageless, therefore timeless; so
we'll leave our heavy, fascinating shadows
on the doorstep; so, I said, we'll simply trace
in unobtrusive strokes what we are now.
You cracked the mystery fish, peeled the caul
from the red crayon of roe – which you gave me.
What part of taste, what part of time is this?
The bathrobe keeps slipping from my shoulders,
but we've been married silver years and gold
– a bare breast would neither shock nor rouse you.
Tell me their names – this fish, this salty planet,
so like and unlike earth, its bright omphalos
a kitchen table. Minutes ago we were strangers,
hours before that, lovers. It's two o'clock
I said in the new language; that's nothing, you said,
your mouth full of scales, that's children's time.

*

We slip into the darkest colour – stillness.
A half-sleep floats like tempera across
our pillows and our limbs, sunk on each other,
and in the dream that blooms from our alignment,
we wake into the rosy corner where
an icon flickers, wake into the icon.
On crimson cloth, the twenty chosen fingers
enact their imperfective verbs of touch.
The child's left hand clasps the maphorion
as it would a stream of hair; his mother's cheek
touches his, and one hand curves a cradle
for the small, uncertain spine; the other, raised,
hushes the infant universe. Dissolving
to a drowse of gold, these two chosen heads,
these twenty fingers, can never say enough,
though laden with the silences of art.

*

The sun was like a diamond. Sleepily
while you worked nearby I tried to hold it
between my eyelids. All the birds were singing
to the sky's cold lavender. I slept again
letting you float – I trusted you to float
not far away. Such brightness trellised us
as if the iconographer had worked
in silver foil and gold, in pearl and turquoise.
The Virgin of the Don, like a czarina
in tear-drop gems and furry velvels, parted
the sky to smile. This was the world of money.
of purchasable grace. I woke and saw
your turned back, the diagrams spread out,
the lamp dipped as an aid to concentration
on slightly displaced, slightly obsolete fact.
Your small, plump, precise hand gripped the ruler
in its mouth, happy as a little dog.
you squinted down and drew a swift straight line.

*

But space is curved, and all who sail in her
– plasmid, bacterium, foetus, curly brain,
the sea. Deep in each other's laps we slept,
well-matched for cradling. One shall never move
without the other, that's the law of nights.
The law of days is – one shall always move
while the other grasps, writhes up, sinks back,
sick as a sturgeon ripped from its spawing-ground
and flung in pouring silver on the heaped
and blushing deck. Only the sturgeon is luckier...
– it makes a single mistake.
We live to lift the glass again, to chase
the flying stillnesses, the mortal icons.

*

In the window lay blue light and other windows;
then there was only the print of this room
on glossy black, with a bare, sickle moon
that seemed to pierce me; now beyond the faint
kitchen glints as far as I can see
there is only black. I could be persuaded
that no moon exists, no trees, no windows
rooted in the round earth, no hope of daylight.
Patience, patience, say the little hearth-gods
smug on your hooks and shelves, unafraid of fire
or servitude – despair is simply one
point of view. And so I try again.
I imagine you travelling beneath the moon
I cannot see, I imagine you moving slowly
into this narrow frame. A greenish dawn
follows you, then the trees, the houses, daylight.
I imagine hope, and hope's redundancy,
our dark silhouette of reunion
like an endless still that vanishes behind
the kissing curtains and the piecemeal snowfall
– after which there is nothing ever after.

*

She waited too; dawn did not bring you home.
Letters were sealed in tears, and crossed. One pleaded.
the other said – impossible. She froze...
The iron echo rings – impossible.
Something she'd read was happening to her:
a train pounding over the wooden bridge
over the frozen lake, and then its windows
slithering like a deck of yellowed cards
down through crashing struts, flames, slopes of ice.
The doors of the water closed. Your letters crossed,
sealed in freezing tears. Everything froze.
She stares up from the bottom of the lake.
The ice has healed smooth as lies, white-faced
as history. Impossible... yet you,
when I look down again, are lying there too.

*

This was my dream. You stood in the doorway
turning the dimmer-switch to a dark glow.
I saw the smiling boy, his butterfly-pause
in the shiny perspex trap, the matted gold
curtain-weave, the junk-shop paperbacks;
then, by the bed, your blue-bond Russian-English
slavar – a daring marriage
of words solemnly trying to mean each other,
telling their secrets in each other's arms.
I woke to the old standing-pool of dawn,
seeing only myself. The light changed,
shook with a breaking tremor...
You were beside me. So it's possible
to be happy, I said, and, in my dream,
I took your warm, lost body to my heart
and nursed my happiness to sleep again.

                    *

Minutes ago we were strangers... Now,
expecting my surprise, you fetch the *vobla*.
Have you forgotten the first taste you fed me?
Our tongues were stiffer, salt was sweeter, then.
You gesture doubtfully, intent on stripping
the fish to a few details of its life:
the papery, jointed pod of the swim-bladder
still tenderly inflated, twisting free,
and now the roe, delicately male
and seaweed-brown, not red as I'd imagined.
What part of light, what part of time is this?
Age, weariness, iconoclasm
watch us for our living salts, our rich
human skins...we swallow the drouth
till nothing's left beyond our lips but scales.
You wouldn't eat them, though I said so once,
wanting the pun, and your dear, careful mouth.

                    *

The boy, so harshly combed and tightly buttoned
into his miniature pin-stripes, looks up
with sparkling gaze and vague, milk-tooth smile,
all-trusting, though a tiny flinch betrays
his sudden, bright, important loneliness.
Somewhere off-camera you are watching him,
moving farther away but watching, watching,
till your eyes bleed with their attempt at filming.
Twenty years later, and you telephone
a birthday greeting, straining to receive
across a shower of crackling stars his tall
uncertain image, and to hear him smile.

*

There was another child, a child of wishes.
Long shadows had fallen, it was late,
but I saw him playing down by shallow water,
his language yours, diminutive, rinsed new.
For a moment, I thought you watched him too,
and the brightness in our eyes was one brightness.

*

I am not the one.
Your fingertips understand it when they blindly
trace my short hair to a little below
the nape of my neck, no further.
I am not the one.
Still they trail onwards, smudging adored soft ghosts.
Dark were they, or light, or in-between?
Ringlets, or straight strands?
Your finger-tips could say, but so much knowledge
cannot translate to our shadow-language, thin
as the paper I write on. Without a past
we'll die to each other, ghost to ghost...
Your fingers mark the stony place.
They are human enough, they search for comfort,
but go on whispering: this is not the one.

*

Into the snowy east of consciousness
your dreams pull sledges, and your eyes are sealed
to keep the future from your wintering heart.
What's sourer than the after-taste of hope,
the nightly vodka at the wrong table,
the wrong attentive gaze? I think of those
who paid their one-way fare in useful lies,
the state turning a crass, wolfish cheek
on which a frail tear announced motherhood.
Is it freedom to forget the life you had,
or to carry it with you like necessity?
The west too is full of snow and whispers,
and if it were a woman it would say:
I had no choice but to disappoint you,
to become the cancelled myth, the ashamed silence,
a word that simply isn't in your language,
a foreign country, even to myself.

*

It was forbidden to destroy an icon.
Although, in time, the jewelled saints fell homesick
and dwindled smokily in mass ascensions,
their charisma remained, and only God,
sighing his aimlessness in moving water,
might wash and wash the remnant to pure nothing.

*

We too have left the life we dared not lose
on the vague strand where history runs in,
cold, innocent, light-fingered. *Goodbye
until the next world,* Zhivago sighed
heroically to his mistress, but we lack
such cheerful metaphysics. Time is all
we ever had: you scarcely treasure it,
and I can only lock it like the ghost
of the present-tense, into these antique rooms.
Better not to have tried to love at all,
perhaps, if this is the only world to love in,
and kinder never to have roused the child
we settled all those years ago to sleep,
if we did so merely to abandon it.

UNCOLLECTED POEMS FROM
SELECTED POEMS
(1987)

Virgil for the Plebs

The child in front of the television set
bends half her mind to a dead language.

Its italics hook her down
between linenboard bent and scarred by generations.

Some progress has been made,
a teacher might say, reporting on the centuries

– a girl, and no patrician,
let loose among the big imperial words;

yet, lacking that substance of self-love
called class, tricked into myth

by special-offer potions for bright hair,
soft-focus studies in the art of kissing,

she's lost her heart for books,
says it's better to marry than learn.

The Trojans and Greeks were fighting over Helen.
Their ships and spears and shields

litter the page, stout but expendable.
Tanks nose across the screen.

Because the wars are in our living-rooms
we think them literature.

We can adjust them, strand the President
in silence, wipe off blood

in the twinking of a switch.
Child-like we gather round for the old stories

of passionate nominatives and accusatives,
or, suddenly quiet, turn up the news to discover

the verb that waits for us
at the end of our sentence.

Two Women

Daily to a profession – paid thinking
and clean hands – she rises,
unquestioning. It's second nature now.
The hours, though they're all of daylight, suit her.
The desk, typewriter, carpets, pleasantries
are a kind of civilisation, built on money,
of course, but money, now she sees, is human.
She has learned giving from her first chequebook,
intimacy from absence. Coming home
long after dark to the jugular torrent
of family life, her smile
cool as the skin of supermarket apples,
she's half the story. There's another woman
who bears her name, a silent, background face
that's always flushed with effort.
The true wife, she picks up scattered laundry,
and sets the table with warmed plates to feed
the clean-handed woman. They've not met.
If they were made to touch, they'd scald each other.

Tides

The other night I slept in a red-roofed village
that was trying not to topple off the land.
Outside the Seamen's Mission a rusty-scaled
cod gasped for coins, standing tip-tailed,
but I turned in at the sign of the Dolphin, where
the landlord drank like a ghost at his own bar,
and his dog barked 'time' in the small hours.
I escaped at dawn to clear my head with the wind
that bounded out across the turfy clay
where at last the moor slipped into the arms of the bay.

Three hundred miles from the pinpoint of a chance
of meeting you, I was perfectly cool.
I watched the sea drag its malevolent, gleaming
tons away from the land it had just darkened,
and was glad I would be cosily south before
it hurtled back to boil at the sea-wall
and unveil a winter, the streets white or streaming,
the mouth of the mission-cod encrusted with ice,
and no one stooping on the pooly sand
to weigh the small cold of a starfish in a warm hand.

When I took the little creature from my pocket
later, I found it had changed shape, as if
in some last, inching retreat from life,
it had been reborn. I placed it in a glass,
freshly filled, with some salt from the breakfast table
– but it didn't stir again. I suppose I'd thought
it might unfurl like a Japanese water-flower,
brimmed with its element. So the foolish hope for
resurrection, or at least the kind of death
that brightens corn-rot to alcohol, driftwood to jet.

All that remained now was a valediction
to tender doubt, and the backward-racing lines
of the railway, sepia after a night of rain,
since I had to come home, leaving the dead starfish
for the landlady, leaving the village
to its history of cod and non-conformist virtue,
and the helpless plunge of its streets to their salty source,
leaving the chastened tourists clambering still
towards the mysteries of some clouded hill;
since I had to trade the rich North Sea for stone;
talk with you, touch you, let the tide turn.

False Wings

The house with its many windows drew the dawn
into itself, and light touched open shapes
and colours – a yellow quilt, our human darkness.
Pillow-grass flowered in all its varieties
– your lashes, soft as charrings, the crisp maze
curling along each forearm,
tiny needles of midnight in your jaw.
By the day's slow brightening,
I discovered the clairvoyance of your eyelids.
They flickered up, even before my lips
had found your sleeping face.
I loved your look of happiness, its pure welcome.
You touched me like your first-born, with a marvelling
sweetness that inventoried each part
and found me whole; yet you touched my heart
most when, climbing our tumult, you took its peak
with the candour of a child
flying into the sun, amazed by falling.

Dark Harvest

They shine like tiny apples, black,
Scented with gin and loneliness,
The easiest fruit, perhaps, to pick
But firm against my tongue's duress
As I interrogate their skin
Kindly, tactfully, knowing that soon
They'll have to break, confess their lies
Of ripeness till my whole mouth cries.

A bush of fruit-lamps burns as clear
In Harrow as in Chistopol.
It brings the life you fled so near
I'm dizzy with its taste and smell.

I wade breast-deep, the whispering bush
Opening up, against my wish,
Those glints and lights I least can bear
– The darkest eyes, the softest hair.

They have survived their altered state,
Your exiled loves. They stir their tea
With teaspoon-clouds of summer fruit,
And test the sweetness patiently.
Your absence falls as light as dust,
Now, on the lives. They're almost used
To swallowing what's dull and cruel:
I think they almost wish you well.

Simple Poem

Why didn't the room say
how long your absence would be,
that night when you climbed the stairs
in your quick, expectant way
and sat across from me?
No word from the lamp or the chair
though they've both been around a bit
and ought to have guessed, not a sign
from the much-used willow plate.
It watched you laugh and eat
and did not seem to care,
as lost in desire as I
– and now you're not here.

And now you're not here, why
must there still be a room
with surfaces that mime
the slow life of the sky,
and a clock to strike off time?
Like an implacable heart
the blind swings open, shut,
on leafy blue, on grey.

Darkness refuses to stay,
and always the numb dawn light
shows a chair, raggedly turned,
and a small lamp that once burned
all through the summer night.
Oh how the light loved then
all the white length of your spine.
My pillow was dark with your hair.
Why doesn't everything die
now you're not here?

Ballad of the Morning After

Take back the festive midnight
Take back the sad-eyed dawn
Wind up that old work ethic
Oh let me be unborn.

After a night of travelling
How can it come to pass
That there's the same tongue in my mouth
The same face in my glass

Same light on the curtain
Same thirst in the cup
Same ridiculous notion
Of never getting up?

Cars stream above the city
The subway throbs below
Whirling a million faces
Like shapeless scraps of snow

And all these melting faces
Flying below and above
Think they are loved especially
Think they especially love

This is a free country
The jails are for the bad
The only British dissidents
Are either poor or mad.

I put my classless jeans on
Open my lockless door
I breathe the air of freedom
And know I'm mad and poor.

Love is the creed I grew by
Love is the liberal's drug
Not Agape but Eros
With his Utopian hug

And in the *close, supportive*
Environment of the bed,
He is liberty, equality,
Fraternity and bread.

That is the supposition
But I say love's a joke
A here-today-and-gone-tomorrow
Childish pinch-and-poke.

Perhaps I'll believe in something
Like God or Politics
I'd build those temples wider
But there are no more bricks.

Some women believe in Sisterhood
They've rowed the Master's ship
Across the lustful silver sea
On his last ego-trip

And some believe in Housework,
And a few believe in Men.
There's only one man that I want,
And I want him again and again.

He sat down at my table.
He finished all the wine.
'You're nothing, dear, to me,' he said,
But his body covered mine,

And stoked the fiery sickness
That's done me to a turn
– The fool that chose to marry
And also chose to burn.

Burning burning burning
I came to self-abuse,
Hoping I'd go blind, but no,
It wasn't any use.

I see a mother and her child
Both turn with starving face.
And that's the story of our lives,
The whole damned human race.

My conscience is a hangover,
My sex-life, chemistry;
My values are statistics,
My opinions, PMT.

Beside my rented window
I listen to the rain.
Yes, love's a ball of iron,
And time, its short, sharp chain.

The middle-aged say life's too brief.
The old and young say 'wrong'.
I'll tell you, if you don't like life,
It's every day too long.

Carpet-Weavers, Morocco

The children are at the loom of another world.
Their braids are oiled and black, their dresses bright.
Their assorted heights would make a melodious chime.

They watch their flickering knots like television.
As the garden of Islam grows, the bench will be raised.
Then they will lace the dark-rose veins of the tree-tops.

The carpet will travel in the merchant's truck.
It will be spread by the servants of the mosque.
Deep and soft, it will give when heaped with prayer.

The children are hard at work in the school of days.
From their fingers the colours of all-that-will-be fly
and freeze into the frame of all-that-was.

Passing a Statue of Our Lady in Derry

She appears tired, though dressed in fresh, white stone,
And bows the bandaged snowdrop of her head
Pleadingly to the bus – which hurries on
And leaves her stranded in my childhood,

Mother of small contritions, great hopes
And the lyric boredom of the rosary
When miracles seemed at our fingertips:
She is much younger now than formerly,

And in her narrow, girlish hands, she weighs
Not holiness, but a frail, human idea
That might accomplish anything – dismiss
An army – or, like childhood, disappear.

A New Song
(for Naim Attallah)

> *Thou feedest them with the bread of tears;*
> *and givest them tears to drink in great measure.*
> PSALM 90

Silences of old Europe
Not even the shofar
Can utter: Maidenek,
Mauthausen, Babi Yar

– Death of the innocent being
Our speciality
Let us add Lebanon's breaking
Sob to the litany.

So many now to mourn for,
Where can the psalmist start?
Only from where his home is,
And his untidy heart.

We pluck our first allegiance
With a curled baby-hand,
Peering between its fingers
To see our promised land;

Yours on a hillside, clouded
With olives; mine a cot
In a London postal district,
Its trees long spilled as soot.

The war was all but over:
It seems my newborn cry
Was somehow implicated
In yells of victory.

But it's the quieter voices
That keep on trying to rhyme,
Telling me almost nothing,
But filling me with shame:

– Germany in the thirties
And half my family tree
Bent to an SS microscope's
Mock genealogy.

Duly pronounced untainted
For his Aryan bride,
My uncle says it's proven
– There are no Jews on our side.

Ancient, unsummoned, shameless,
The burdens of prejudice:
All through my London childhood,
Adults with kindly eyes

Muttered the mild opinions
So innocently obscene
(Hitler was not 'all stupid',
and 'not all Jews are mean').

Later, the flickering movie;
Greyish, diaphanous
Horrors that stared and questioned:
Has God forgotten us?

Oh if our unborn children
Must go like us to flame,
Will you consent in silence,
Or gasp and burn with them?

It is so late in the century
And still the favourite beast
Whines in the concrete bunker
And still the trucks roll east

And east and east through whited
Snowfields of the mind
Towards the dark encampment;
Still the Siberian wind

Blows across Prague and Warsaw,
The voices in our head
Baying for a scapegoat:
Historians gone mad;

Thugs on a street corner,
The righteous gentile who
Pins Lebanon like a yellow star
To the coat of every Jew.

Silences of old Europe
Be broken; let us seek
The judgement of the silenced,
And ask how they would speak.

Then let the street musician
Crouched in the cruel sun
Play for each passing, stateless
Child of Babylon,

Conciliatory harmonies
Against the human grain,
A slow psalm of two nations
Mourning a common pain

– Hebrew and Arabic mingling
Their single-rooted vine;
Olives and roses falling
To sweeten Palestine.

Winter Borscht

Don't look for spies or angels in our kitchen:
We're Christmassing far from all religions.
Utopia doesn't mean a thing to us
And we've forgotten how to talk with children.

Eating, though, continues. And ever since
I dipped my spoon into this wavy, scarlet
Winter sun, lifted its cap of beet-leaves,
I've felt as festive as a wedding taxi

Climbing in clouds of exhaust, frost, ribbons,
With a bride who'll simply giggle and take snaps
(The sandy, pointed beard, implacably growthless
Under its arc-light, needn't expect a visit).

Then, of course, it's back to the revolution,
The tasteless sundae casting turd-like shadows,
And not enough spoons, and too many elbows.
Invited, after all, to the state banquet,

I think about God again, and the Christian *chutzpah*
Of those who made His textbook so alive,
You could hear the jostle of wings, the musical pings,
And see the haloes' glare, from Florence to Kiev.

They too loved red. In fact, their rosy seraphs
Were here before us, bowed towards our plates.
Look, they've left us both a golden sign,
A faint, indelible, blood-stained halo-print.

At Kibbutz Amiad

These are the solid texts
– houses in white lanes
scribbled with jacaranda.
But it's in the margins

we'll find our poems
said footloose Mandelstam.
I weigh this as you sleep
and all the kibbutzim

of the Upper Galilee
grow moody with children
escaping vaguely home,
tired as the khamsin.

Quarrels, piano practice
– nothing is lonelier
in this story of families
than our marginalia.

We keep ourselves to ourselves
in a flower-shadowed house
with an empty second bedroom
that cannot fathom us.

Camouflage

Hot Rhine-Valley days, the misty odours
of pollution and Late Romanticism;
hubris on a meagre city beach
where I am burning my base self to gold,
shifting with the sun as it slyly escapes
at an odd, foreign angle, never overhead,
thinking it something like our conversations
in the tongue we cannot share, haunting, oblique:

twilights that whirr with home-flying bicycles
and a perennial, anxious excitement
in case the night should betray its incredible promise
– for we are moody and unverifiable
chameleons of a thousand joys and troubles;
parted by so much daylight, we might arrive
at our violet-skied, electric meeting-place
as strangers who must touch each other's skin
over and over, and still not quite remember:

night, and the reading is from Dostoyevsky.
Your new voice, fiery, rough, argumentative,
astounds the room, I dare not look at your face,
until at last the flare of language dies,
dies back to the dark garden
of breath and watching. Sunlight glares from my skin
like a confession, but my secrets are white.
You comment on my 'distinctive markings'
as I home towards you through the branching shadows,
fierce and intent, in perfect camouflage.

Eclipses

Midday. The earth holds its breath,
the shadows can't move an inch.
Only the sky seems to be rushing away.
It vanishes into the blue of its furthest blue,
dropping a little curled handful of sun-smeared iris
onto the world for us.
The poppies are clear glass bowls of some inky night-cap,
the grass, an amazement of light.
And you and I, what are we,
our soft, random collision
eclipsing us in this garden,
this room? Pass your hand
quickly over the sun's brow and invent
a glowing midday dusk
where I shall undress to my ear-studs
and you, to nothing. Where the exotic, slow,
brachiating animal we evolve,
time-lapsed, will have no name,
and I'll press my lips by mistake to my own skin.

Second Lives

Wedging himself by degrees
through the unlatched door,
the foundling tom cat

with his double set of neuroses
looks at the woman in bed,
decides he needn't leave.

They listen to the plug
knuckling the wall's far side,
then the granular buzz

of coffee-beans spinning
into fragments of themselves,
truer than themselves.

Around her stand the dead,
risen as usual,
encumberings of teak

veneer, uncut moquette,
thin brass and sprigged plastic
glooming in the dawn

of her second life.
The man who left that crumpled
space on her right,

chose them carefully.
She knows in which junk-shops
and at what price.

He was by himself,
breathing in the strong essence
of private ownership,

tongue-tied and stateless
as the tense face that dodged him
from mirror to speckled mirror.

This is his second country;
she, his lost wives;
she is twenty, thirty, forty

as she waits for him to bring
the Oxfam tray
with its dusty wicker plait

and scribble of poppies.
He'll set it gently down
on the quilt's collapsing flesh,

and, stepping back to watch
her childish pleasure, taste
the day's first sip with her.

A Woman of a Certain Age

'This must have been my life
but I never lived it.'
– Her childishly wide stare
at some diminishing reel
of space and brightness, half
illusory, half not,
stuns to an epitaph.
And I can read it all:
how a little lie
whitened to twenty years;
how she was chosen by
something called happiness,
yet nothing, nothing was hers.
And now she has to turn
away, and her bruised eyes
are smiling in their nets:
'It's simple, isn't it?
Never say the yes
you don't mean, but the no
you always meant, say that,
even if it's too late,
even if it kills you.'

The Last Day of March

The elms are darkened by rain.
On the small, park-sized hills
Sigh the ruined daffodils
As if they shared my refrain
– That when I leave here, I lose
All reason to see you again.

What's finishing was so small,
I never mentioned it.
My time, like yours, was full,
And I would have blushed to admit
How shallow the rest could seem;
How so little could be all.

In the Craft Museum

Some nations lock up their poets. Ours have the key
to a high, clean room labelled *Sensibility*.

They have sat there now for a very long time,
and are clearly no threat to a democratic regime.

They are old, of course, but remarkably unspoiled;
their edges still cut, their moving parts are oiled.

Of course, they're permitted to go down to the street,
and the street may visit them, if it wipes its feet.

Here comes the guide now, telling the solemn young faces
that, yes, the poets still work, but don't touch the glass cases.

Weeds

In gardens, it's the unwanted
babies that grow best and biggest,
swarming our beds of frail
legitimate darlings with roots
like wire and crude, bright flower-heads.

They seem oblivious
of the fury of steel prongs
earthquaking around them.
If they fall today, tomorrow
they'll stand all the greener.

Too soon, the beautiful lives
we've trembled over with sprays
of pesticide, friendly stakes,
and watering-cans at sunset,
give in, leaving us helpless.

The weeds, the unfavoured ones,
stare at us hungrily,
and since it is hard to live
empty of love, we try
to smile; we learn to forgive them.

FROM **THE GREENING OF THE SNOW BEACH**

(1988)

The Flood of Silence

What killed Pushkin was not D'Anthes' bullet;
what killed him was lack of air.
BLOK

What a Devil's Trick that I should be born
with a soul and talent in Russia.
PUSHKIN

On London nights, Decemberish, icy,
When streets and sky and Thames are all
One shimmering bale, gold-sequinned, pricey;
When the wind hardens to a wall
On corners where theatres glitter,
And words are tossed away like litter
While golden eggs lay pizza-chains
And burger-bars and video-games,
I think of you in Tsarskoye Selo
Writing your ode to Liberty;
Bliss was it in that dawn to be
A dreamy, radical young fellow
Saved from Yakutsk, if not from court.
By exile of a milder sort.

I think how silence spreads its rivers
Over unstable, swampy banks;
Even the bronze-wrapped horseman shivers
As bridges float away in planks.
A wave shins up a lamp-post's rigging;
First doors, then balconies are swigging
The muddy water, then the chimes
Of plump St Isaac's; on it climbs...
Miraculously, we can hear you
Still, as if you were a bird –
Art with an olive-sprig – absurd
Image that surely fails to cheer you
As you gaze out of Leningrad,
Your mausoleum, huge and sad.

You built your ark, although the rising
Flood was almost at your throat –
A speedy, shapely, un-capsizing
Twentieth-century language-boat;
But still the future's uncreated
And writers with an elevated
Sense of buoyancy tend to drown
In deaths as airless as your own.
Brave actor, forced to play the gallant
When, in that proud, possessive place,
Adultery giggled in your face,
You died, having bemoaned your talent,
In shallow rivers of your blood –
Though you survive the greater flood.

The Duchess and the Assassin

The Grand Duchess Yelizaveta
Worried about the troops in Manchuria
While Sergei went on crushing the Revolution
In his silk-lined German carriage.

That afternoon of the palace sewing-bee
She was thinking about men's shirts,
Not of the bodies that might break in them,
Proving her perfect seams incontinent.

She watched the lazy bouncing
Of vulturish wrists, and knew it was for the best
That her mind should simply float...
She had drawn out the needle again –

The cotton had the strong pull of sunlight –
When the day went up like the Tsar's fleet at Tsushima.
She flung down the shirt and ran
Straight for the flushed smoke-cloud: silk and skin.

She picked up what she recognised
As the Governor-General, thinking: 'not my husband.'
Her apron sagged with the enormity...
The blood on her thighs screamed like birth-blood.

Clothes, after that, were water; even flesh
Showed her its inmost threading.
She sat, untouchable, by the opened curtains,
Burning her eyes on a lifetime of unpicking.

At last she came to the prison,
To the windowless cell, the stink of certainty.
She wanted to know why.
Even terrorists had their reasons.

He was nervous, and tried to sneer.
She felt her power. She wanted to lift her finger
To singe the skin of his cheek.
You don't understand. Forgiveness

Is the last thing I need, he said.
So you'll hang, Iván, she said.
His smile cleared: but the cause will outlive us both!
And she thought of the ripped halves

Of a shirt, stitched together
In stringy blood – two deaths,
Seamless, that Russia would wear
When it came to bury her.

Note: The Grand Duchess Yelizaveta was the sister-in-law of Tsar Nicholas II, and the wife of the Governor General of Moscow, Sergei Alexandrovich, who was as universally disliked as she was admired. The Governor General was assassinated at the Kremlin Gates by the Socialist Revolutionary, Ivan Kalyayev, on 4 February 1917.

A Memo About the Green Oranges

They sat like a disarmament proposal
On our table in the hotel dining-room,
Looking less and less negotiable.
Even the vegetarians flinched from them.

The Talks beside the lake weren't going well.
Neither was the turnover in these
Miniature ballistic atrocities –
Which now began to occur at every meal.

Oranges Are Orange. Grass Is Green –
Like policemen's greatcoats. Never Trust A Red.
(It's better to be dead than dyed that shade.)
You Can't Tell A *Sosiska* By Its Skin...

But what about an orange? Feeling less
Hopeful than thirsty on Sadóvaya Street
One day, I bought a mossy half-a-kilo.

The Geneva Talks stand just as still, or stiller,
And this is simply a memo, a PS,
To say those green-skinned oranges are sweet.

The Fire-Fighter's Widow
on her First Memorial Day Outing

We ride in the hired coach
North through April grey.
Spinneys of frail birch
Stagger up through the snow
Still rucked along the highway
As it rolls towards endless Moscow –
Nothing much else. We try
To lose ourselves in the view;
Pressed to our own faces,

We watch them travel with us,
Sickly, shut-out, like ghosts.
It was twelve months ago
That day our air was lit
Hugely and blown apart,
And still some people say –
Though they're not supposed to know –
Death hasn't gone away.

We're far, far North of green.
I'm glad to be so far,
Though they say the crops are clear
And plentiful this year,
I don't want to go near
Whatever our lives were then,
Between the rushing Pripyat
And the lake which never froze.
How warm and clean it was,
That water as it lapped
The broad towers of the plant –
Water that swept and cooled
The sun-packed rods, and kept
A little of their gold.
We fished (the fish were fat,
Sun-lazy), swam and dreamed.
Uranium was our friend
Until we forgot to fear it.
That was the night it turned.
The lake shrank in its heat;
Above the towers the air
Poured in savage plumes
As if the sun had been thrown
Earthwards. *His* grave is there.

He was a hero. We,
Therefore, are hero wives,
Trudging through burnt-out lives
And finding less and less,
However patiently
We stir the ash.
Pensioned, re-housed, redressed
By this Memorial Day
We wipe our eyes to say

None of it means a thing.
Surely our country's smashed
More heroes than it's worth?
I hate its giant hand
Which gathers men like clay
And moulds them into masses
To build red victories with.
They should have counted ten
Before they dashed away
And rose above the furnace,
Thinking they had to fling
Their lives down with the sand
In order to be men.

A Western scientist, one
Of those who built the Bomb,
In later life admitted
'I didn't think. I did
Experiments.' He's dust,
Now, in a Christian tomb,
And small as his regrets,
But if there was a God
Perhaps he'd be hauled back
Somehow across the years,
And made to ride with us.
He'd see what hope still is:
Our children, picnics, tears,
Our cheap new dresses, black:
He'd see the white graves
That now gleam into view,
Cleaner than any snow –
And leave the rest undone.

No other cemetery
Is quite as new as this –
The unplanted burial-ground
Of a spaced-out century.
There's no eternal flame
(As if they thought a glimpse
Of flame could drive us mad),
Only carnations, red
And dark as the burrowing
Roots of the meltdown.

Uniforms guide us through
Our public sorrowing.
Speeches drip their vowels
Through the muddy afternoon
Like ruined icicles.
We are praised, and shepherded.

Under us lie the dead
Heroes we used to know.
We watched them as they changed
Inside their unmarked skin –
Their useless, shivering courage,
Their shame as they vomited.
In a tangle of thick vines
All the good essences –
Saline, bone-marrow, blood –
Streamed down to rescue them
But sank in the rotting web
Of burning they'd become.
We touched them through our gloves,
Felt nothing. When they died
We were relieved. And then
Relief seemed out of date –
Like happiness, an echo
From life-times ago
When death was still a child,
Before it learned to breed.

We are the heroes' wives.
We are decaying too.
Some kneel beside the graves
Forgetting what they know –
That the world is a carelessness,
A chance in a universe.
Some weep. I'm not like these.
I simply walk away
And walk away, and then
The circle seems to close,
I'm back where I began,
Looking down in dismay
At the grass, the flowers, my shoes.

Leningrad Romance

1 *A Window Cut by Jealousy*

Not far from the estuary's grey window
They lit cigarettes and talked. Water kept meeting stone,
Lips kept sticking to paper, time kept burning.
The lilacs were burning down to the colour of stone.
She said, I was born here, I've lived here always.
Stone kept moving in water, time kept burning,
Smoke became palaces, palaces faded and faded.
My home's in Moscow, he said, my wife and children...
Perhaps they are just the white ash-fall of night,
Perhaps they are stone. Stone kept looking at shadows,
Shadows died in the white ash-fall of night.
Water kept playing with windows, time kept burning,
Fingers played with the burning dust of the lilacs,
The palaces faded and faded. I've lived here always,
She said, I've friends in Moscow. Thoughts became palaces,
Time went out, hands became estuaries,
The estuary was the colour of dying lilac.
They talked and lit cigarettes. Shadows flowed over the table.
They fingered them, but they didn't notice mine,
Not far from the estuary's grey window.

2 *Safe Period*

He will unlock the four-hooked gate of her bra,
Not noticing a kremlin of patched cotton,
With darkening scorch-marks where her arms press kisses.
She will pull back her arms, disturbing drifts
Of shallow, babyish hair, and let him drink,
Breathless, the heavy spirit smell, retreating
At length with a shy glance to grasp the chair-back,
And, slightly stooped, tug out the darker bandage.
Her cupped palm will glow as she carries it
Quickly to the sink, like something burning.
He sees the bright beard on each inner thigh,
Carnations curling, ribboning in the bowl.
Her hands make soapy love. The laundered rag
Weeps swift pink tears from the washing-string.
He's stiffened with a shocked assent. She breathes
Against him, damp as a glass. A glass of red vodka.

Finding the Sun

On Vasilievsky Island, brown and rumpled
With tramlines, stone in all its dreamed canals,
And plots still whispering through its plywood walls
I thought of the sun which Mandelstam had buried
In Petersburg, in the *velvet Soviet night*
And knew it lived, under the people's feet.

Wherever they trod, damp walkway planks or cobbles,
The crowds in their furry earflaps were trampling a thaw.
Rocks of soiled water loosened themselves
From the lips of drainpipes; soon, they'd dash for the river.
Spring's muddy pools would flower and the people know
That the time was ripe for exposing fragile earlobes.

In the meantime they went about hugged to themselves.
I thought of boats, their iron skirts swarming down
To the harbour-bed, lodging an iceberg's depth
Against a rusting anchor's mud-sunk sickle.
Dogged, they dreamed in queues, or butted the wind
Over bridges and through the arcades of Gostiny Dvor.

Darkness softly wrapped the great, flowing rush-hour
And still they were dawning and homing, those platoons,
Surging on their inscrutable manoeuvres.
They poured up from the burial pit of the metro
Like pyramid-builders, yoked by necessity.
Yet I saw how some had a secret happiness:

The militiaman in his heavy, mossy coat
Held a box of Napoleon pastry by its string
Daintily as a child's hand; a grey-faced woman
Lulled with her breath an armful of red carnations.
And in all the palaces rackety lifts crept up
Into night and the gleam of doors, bright-medalled with locks.

I sniffed a dialect, then, of *savoury pies,*
Pancakes, the evening samovar, soft sighs
And warm shawls and a hot stove to sleep on:
And the speeches lengthened, irremediable
In the lonely, jarring light of television –
But everyone wedged a chair in at the table.

Measured vistas, the seamless welding of Rome
And Byzantium in gold as thin as skimmed milk,
Cannot contain the skyline of their hope.
It sinks and flickers, looking for depth, for stone,
And this is the point it rests at. Vasilievsky –
Where the poets will meet again and find the sun.

Quotations from Mandelstam, *Tristia*, and Dostoyevsky, *Crime and Punishment.*

A West Country Twin-Town

In the new year of our new life together
    When, dreamy, diffident
As stuttering English snow, we stole each other
    From history's Janus-glare,
And then, to cure our failure of intent,
    Glanced at a map, drove west
Towards the refuge of that kindest city –
    Fathered by Rome, but a true Hellenist,
Whose naiad waters, glorying in their own
    Warm, emerald climate, try to wash the frown
From marble rectitude: in that new year

A birch tree sidled up to welcome us
    Plaintively, a skinny city peasant
Sighing the forest wasn't what it was,
And we, lounging in bed at noon, could count
    Through snow-dim glass a row
Of colonnades or pan-pipes, not convinced,
But happily suspecting that the pleasant
    Angel of English fantasy had swished
    Her wing across our view:
So we were held until the room went dark,
And vision sank to a shady glow of flesh...
    But midnight, scathing as a Bolshevik
Of love's imperial privacies, burst in
    And flung us out to public life again.

By one o'clock the city was a mess,
    Silent and slumped after the ritual shrieks
To *auld lang syne*, and dangerously chilled:
Even her dreams were limestone, moist and cold.

In that new year that wasn't a new start,
    Simply its shadow which, when lost,
Might still seem solider than all the rest,
    We watched grey water shrug itself along
In ruffled furs, and the mosquito snow
    Hugged by a ring of lamplight as it danced.
So deeply cold the sleeping city grew
    Each night that I believed her comatose,
Deaf to her naiads, fatally entranced.
    Even the Renault seemed about to die;
Curled like a mercury-ball, a frozen mouse,
It could not raise a spark, but coughed
    With wincing shoulders, frail, tubercular,
While, from your rag-bound thumb, a hot, red tear
    Was futile, like all human sacrifice.

I was prepared never to get away:
    Now that you'd told me where we might have been,
I'd come to think that it was where we were,
    And every street could float off into sea.
Your 'most-premeditated' city, scarved
    In tremulous rivers, numberless bloodstreams,
    And yet unable to escape its dreams,
Had locked us into one stern homesickness,
    So even when we freed ourselves, our roads
    Would always take us north, and Bath appear
In memory's closing window like the ghost
    Of Petersburg at the start of each new year.

FROM **FROM BERLIN TO HEAVEN**
(1989)

From Berlin to Heaven

1 *Democracy at the Burgerbraukeller, 1926, 1984*

We just walked in
And found the moment where
Enormous amber waves
Run beautifully over
The map of soiled empties
And history's remade.
Apprentice Hitler
Jumps on a table,
Trenchcoat-belt frisking
Like a clawed, clumsy tail.
He shoots the ceiling
– A Michelangelo
From the heavy suburbs
Where art is caricature.
Stage dandruff sifts
Onto uniforms, suits.
The patrons still don't know
Whether salvation dances
In such smeared boots.
They study surfaces
Especially those that wink
And brim their glasses
– Worth ninety Marks a sip.
When the order comes
To carry on drinking,
Up go a thousand suns.
The chairs scratch and clap
The floorboards' backs,
And full throats roar
How they will always be
For hops and barley
Whoever's yelling 'Time'
At the pantheon
From below an aproned lip.
He shrinks a little now.
He's almost Chaplinesque
But not incredible

(And not quite charmless)
– His glance could quickly pierce
Us where we sit.

2 *Munich*

Utopia – nowhere
I ever knew
Until that morning.
We had left the sleeper
Blackly streaming
South like an *anschluss*,
A riderless nightmare.
I was still wishing
Vienna, Vienna,
As her breath touched me.
She was pure city
And her brightening forth
In the moment between
Waking and blinking
The heavy gold-dust
Out of my surmise
Was familiar as only
A constant hope is.
We called her 'München',
Tender with surprise.

A sixties child
In a fire-touched brocade,
She curtseyed across
The Marian sky.
If she had willed
Her forgetfulness,
We couldn't blame her.
We too were wide-eyed,
We too, faintly poisoned.
As the day withdrew,
She possessed us differently.
Her shadow found you
And the catch in her voice
Was the buried grace note
Of the Slav.

She turned and turned
Her Russian face
And I heard her whisper
– Extinguishing, enchanting –
Of divorce and marriage
It is divorce
Cuts the deeper heartline:
There can be no future
That is not his past.

Bound to this course,
One night we sat
In futurist Odeonplatz.
Islanded, water-dazzled
Lorelei,
We softly murdered
A song of the people.
Our thin strophes
Were the circles where
A mail-coach butterflied
With its snow-faced driver.
As the storm encrystalled
His upturned room
And kneeling horses
To the arched, brilliant silence
Of a polar tomb,
He dreamed a letter home
And his blood-sugar, sinking
Slowly to zero,
Saw him through
To the death-drowsy, solemn,
Last 'I kiss you'.

Perhaps the blur, stinging
Our eyes, was him.
Beyond us, too,
Lay distances,
Blanked by longing,
And, beyond these,
Expectantly
Fading towards us,
The radiance of footprints
We had each called 'family',

And betrayed.
And then I thought
Of a place too small
Even to spell,
A broken star
Where the map creased.
It blazed in the glare
Of an island's crime
Against her continent.
But we went on singing
Until history fell
In easy shadows
At the city's feet
And *peace in our time,*
Our breath said, peace
In our time.

3 *Jerusalem*

From our window on the third floor
We look down through glass
Into the wakeful restaurant,
Its roof thinly strewn
With rushes, soldier dolls
Pressing their olive knees
Together under the tables.
The tables streaming outwards,
Meeting the competition,
Dissolving in it.
So God diversifies
Into many fields
And some are bloodless.
He can be worshipped here
By sitting stunned and bright
As a shekel in the glare
Of the rival videos.
Their howling close-ups swim
The blue desert night,
Box-office Ayatollahs
Irresistible as sex
And disappointment.

But they are not our drama.
I move from the window
To see how far you've travelled,
To touch the thread
That drew you tense and sinking
Into the clotted weave
Of snow, birch-forest, blood,
And, severed, drifts you back
To your first estranging.
We've slouched, letting our fingers
Creep in each other s pockets
On the Via Dolorosa,
And drunk pure alcohol,
Obtainable all over Zion
From any mirage.
Perhaps that's why you seem
So far from me, so small.
Above the double bed
The air shakes violently,
Becoming water.
As the fan turns its face
First to one, then to the other,
I ask for the last time
The impure but essential question
'Who did you love the most?'
And this is Jerusalem
And so you have to answer
And so the word is made flesh
That will stare at us all summer.

4 *Masada*

There was one god
Too huge to bury.
We crawl in his frown.
Its lumps and pleats
Ache against
A small, cruel sun.
If sacrifice
Is necessity
And we honour those
Whose blood was teased out

Like a tress of crimson
River from rock,
Should we admire
A truck or plane
That assumes the form
Of a burning bush?

Our cable-car
Shivers, sinks.
Better to say
We're in god's hands
Though his fingers are nothing
But wings and prayers.
We're looking down
On an aftermath:
The sleepy lips
Of the dunes parting
Over steel thumbs:
Transfiguration's
Eye-blink, then
An ash of visions
Where the sky touched Gehenna,
Where we were human
For the last time.

The earth is sweet
But a tar path
Sends us in scalded
Leaps to the sea
And that grainy chair
Is comfortless
As Jordan's arm
Round Israel's shoulder.
Seraphim walk,
Piercing, careless,
All over us.
We hang and hear
The tablets gasp
As a flung bottle
Bursts with commandments:
To be soul
To be salt
To be sky
To be skin
– To be stripped of it.

Guiltlessly loitering
On what may well be the site
Of a future excavation
– Easy to date
By the pale, immortal,
Wave-buckled bleach-bottle,
And the shadow that was us –
It's good to face south,
An ice-age drizzling
To bronze in the tumbler
With its ghost-kiss of a mouth
From the age of refrigeration.
A roof is vital for this
– One, perhaps, which hums
With beetle-work
And a young vine's distillation
In radiant leaves and topplings
Of cloudless, skin-tight bubbles.
It must be knitted well
With shady minuses
To cool a skull too thinly
Served for its own yolk.
Then, after the blandishments
Of the zinc-top table,
The Asian jig, jangled
On a microchip's pinhead,
And the last, clean rock-fall,
There must be sea.
Superlative exile
From star-nests more remote
Than Copernicus,
Teasing the absolute
We wish on her,
She dissembles mildly
As a picnic cloth, stained
By immortal feasting,
With deeps and wind-plains
Of every conceivable turquoise.
From such a posting,
Hallucinatory

Beyond the captioned glow
We first reclined in,
We can detect the sun
At his daily confidence trick,
The elegant, coasting
Style that suggests progress
But is closer to suspension
– Busy, myopic
As any firing mind.
In the tangible sphere
Long thought inferior,
Earth's patient wash-day,
Hand over hand beneath
The hilly froth,
Is visibly everything
We're boiling down to
– With diminishing hope.
Zephyrs and Vespas,
Winking on the tongue
Of wine-dark bitumen
Waspishly ape
That losable art of horizons.
They surge and drown
In Procrustean silences.
The corpses too,
Chalky or rosy, matt
Or gloss, are mere burlesque,
A miniature send-up
Of high catastrophe.
They lay themselves out,
Thieved pinches of ozone
Scenting the orifices
Where, as the heart stills,
Life, with any luck,
Will open again
Its friendly, crawling eyes
In diamond multiples.
Though light's their element,
These simpler retinas
Are hooded now
With the horrible, peeled blindness
Of statues, approached

Too closely in peopled rooms.
But imagine how
Richly millennial
The stone imagination!
Ours is no different.
Peep-holes compressed
To their shivering fringes,
It gorges on blackness
And dappled fire-squalls,
While a beq more radiation
Than flesh can bear
Frisks the astonished cells
Of a naked marble breast.

6 *Hypothesis*

In Heaven, it's said, we meet
Our relatives. And so,
Love being the thickest, brightest
Of all the body fluids,
I must look forward to
My three handshakes with his past.
Leaving him ungreeted,
We'll take a step closer
To hold each other at arm's-length,
Utter the names we fear.
We'll add the dates and places
Of each attachment, sworn
To keep beyond time and place.
There will be competition
At first, manoeuvres.
But slowly we'll learn
How innocent we are.
Heaven has to exist
If only for people like us
– Haunted, ambiguous,
A veiled colony,
A broken sisterhood.
It is our one chance
To read beyond his eyes
From the mixed grain of our hair,
From the tiny stars of our skin,

To our complicity.
We shall launder our differences
In the strong river of tears
Whose end is sunlight.
And I shall let him go
To each one as she was
In all her young desire
When I was less to him
Than London on the blue
Globe he revolved
With slow-burning fingers
Away from the known world.

Our Early Days in Graveldene

Houses eat money, even council houses.
Ours was officially a *maisonette*.
It was first in a block of twelve, its shiplap coat
Still neat and almost white. We were 49.
Not far from a box of a pub, The Bunker's Knob

– Named for some veteran's clopping wooden leg.
Each cul-de-sac spoke rustic legends: Foxwood,
Broombank, The Grove. I worked on the inside
Where everything could change. I glossed the stairs
Orange. Orange for hope and happy children.

I had two friends in Graveldene, both *Elaines*.
Big Elaine moaned about her hips and her husbands.
As we queued for the bus, she'd shift their weight with sighs.
I used to sit in the summer with Little Elaine,
Drinking Coke on her rust-streaked balcony.

She looked too young to have children, and too small.
I was scared sick when her toddler swung the kitten.
He's killing it, I cried. She wasn't bothered.
She smiled with her own kitten-face, creamy, cruel.
I thought of battered babies, I couldn't help it.

There was Stell the single mother, Rose the widow
– Women who worked and were always dashing out
For cod and chips. There was the Rasta, Cyril,
Who slashed his throat that time the bailiffs came.
When they came to us we hid behind the door.

They pushed through a folded paper, promising us
Distraint of Property. Oh boy, we simply
Had to laugh. One mattress, several prams,
A high-chair for the eldest, a rush-mat
Half-way to Shredded Wheat, and the transistor.

'All you need is love,' sang the druggy Liverpool voices.
We knew by then they weren't singing for us
And that love ate money, just as houses did.
The sixties were dying, starved for LSD
In the mines and factories, on estates like ours.

We split up in the end. We've done all right.
Sometimes we meet. The other day he said,
'I drove round Graveldene just for a look,
And the door of 49 was off its hinges.
I went inside. I saw your orange stairs.'

Wealth

One Christmas we'd have said 'Rovaniemi'
And bounced in lightly on an Arctic tail-wind
To see the sleigh parked on the airport roof.

I would have steadied you on your first skis
Between the clotted fields, and sent you sailing,
Inarguable brightness overhead,
The clean, etched groove ice-hard in front of you.

A Geometry Lesson for the Children of England

1 *The Triangle*

You wanted the cymbals.
  A fat boy got those.

You wanted the side-drum.
  The prefect got that.

You wanted the tambourine.
  A pretty girl got that.

You wanted the maracas.
  A black girl got those.

You wanted to be the conductor.
  You got the triangle.

It's very important to count
  When you've got the triangle.

If you make a mistake
  It sings 'mistake'

In a tiny voice, shameless,
  Above the rest.

The conductor jabs her stick.
  The band lurches on

To the big crescendo.
  Light winks from the silver tubes.

Your chance was trembling towards you
  Why did you forget to count?

2 *A Lesson on the Uses of the Instruments*

What is the protractor?
  A boat no a half of melon
  Says the silly child's pencil

What is the set-square
  A ski-slope whoosh here I go
  Says the silly child's pencil

What is the compass?
  A roundabout just for me
  Says the silly child's pencil

And when you've finished playing
  Says the teacher, snatching the compass
  A bayonet

3 *The Circle*

You choose the dissenting circle
– The one that fits your head
Exactly, and most of your heart.

How comfy to sit in a circle
So nice, your hands ring-a-rosy
With other, like-minded hands.

146

You chant the high principles
And thė quiet rage of your circle
As if they were 'Three Blind Mice'.

Do you know what to sing next?
Do you always know what to sing next
When you sit in the right circle?

4 *More Triangles*

The isosceles triangle
Is lofty and refined
Like our democracy

The scalene triangle
Goes its own sweet way
Like our democracy

The equilateral triangle
Is fair as fair can be
Like our democracy

The obtuse triangle
Seems to have fallen asleep

A Lawn for the English Family

I did not invent this garden
though I put the children in it.
I was not its ruler. I wanted
only pity and beauty to rule it.

Fat dahlias rule it now
and small, flushed fish, strategic
in their twisted pool,
aiming their confidences.

All will be sucked back
into the light one day
and you'll see the eternal law,
the dictatorship of green.

No whisper will shield the rose
in her fevered return to nature,
nor the infant pimpernel
who foresees the weather.

Like an official broadcast
the untaught mouths
of convolvulus spatter white
on tangling wires.

There is a room in the corner
that has crawled out here to die
and the apple tree hugs its only
apple, its shrivelled soul.

Can you see them at last
swimming the leaves? They are children
who were thrown on the world's mercies,
who were unendurable.

Neither the state nor the state school
nor the solitary jungle-gym
purchased by mail order
could teach them the finished trick

of emergence and escape.
At first, though, they climb quickly.
Their sandals squeak on metal
warm from their hands and the sun.

For a while they can sit in the sky,
laughing at money, its blades
on all sides, slicing and scouring
the shapes of pity and beauty.

Jarrow

Nothing is left to dig, little to make.
Night has engulfed both firelit hall and sparrow.
Wind and car-noise pour across the Slake.
Nothing is left to dig, little to make
A stream of rust where a great ship might grow.
And where a union-man was hung for show
Nothing is left to dig, little to make.
Night has engulfed both firelit hall and sparrow.

Above Cuckmere Haven
(for John Burningham)

This is a reachable coast:
The cliff, though it unscrolls
The modest curve of a buttress,
Is no young Atlas
And doesn't presume to try
Shouldering up the sky

– And the sky itself,
Translucent as a harebell,
Pales, but will not disclose
The point at which it wavers,
Becomes an immortelle
Of gases, stars.

The forsaken pillboxes
Doze in their rust,
No patriotic gull
Wooingly calls
The farm-boys to enlist;
Though the air seems prodigal

With ghostly fires again,
These are the grandchildren
Who never went to the Somme,
Dunkerque or Spain,
But packed the silos dumb
With missile-grain.

Visions, like meadow-blues,
Are dust in the hand,
Seed where the grass thins
To light, and where the cliff
Perishes, chalk and sand:
This is a coast of bones.

What remains is a view:
The cliff, upswept from the beach
And the drying threads of the mere,
Lifting whitely two
Crumbling wings, on which
Other wings briefly appear.

The First Strokes
Letter to a friend learning English

Before he died, my father drowned in silence.
I thought of him just now, writing to you
In my head about the sea – that medicinal light
I longed to rush to your city of rooms and deadlines,
Your lost July – since it was he who taught me
To swim. In any sea he was stylish, fluent.
He knew its idioms, loved its argument.
So, when my four-year-old, his adventuring grandchild,
Slipped her hold on a wet rock, dropped speechless
Into the swell, he plunged and rescued her.
She used to tell us how huge fish came leering,
Making eyes at her as she bubbled down;
Now what she likes to remember are the hands
That drove apart the soupy green, and calmly
Scattered her suitors, saved her for the sun.

It was, soon after this I led him to the pool:
I made him teach me. And, in half an hour,
I had left his side, was lazily at home
In the deepest water, thinking I'd always known how.
It was as simple as doing what he told me
– An obedience I could never risk as a child.
By the time he lost language, I had almost learned ·
To talk to him. He studied dictionaries
At first with an embarrassed grin, then frowning,
And the deep words we could have plumbed together
Ran white. I thought of all this, writing a blue
Letter about the sea, wanting to coax you
Into the tongue you almost know, but fear,
Having come so late to its stories; wanting to say
That the strokes of an English sentence are easy, requiring
Only a little self-trust as you kick off
From the margin and glide towards me, sensing all round you
The solid, patient, unbreakable arm of the water.

After an Emigration

To cut free of the past is not very hard.
You must do it quickly, fall
Absolutely into the offered hand or city.
The past is light, the past is obedient.
It spins from its severed moorings into nowhere.
Only gradually from nowhere it returns.

First it's a dream, at length, a door, open.
Ironical, you appraise
From every angle that city or that person
Not, after all, so bright, free, fascinating
That you were spared the poignant recognitions.
A face floats back. It's yours. You become yourself.

You exist daily on the one thought:
Not that the past was any better than this
But that this is no better than the past.

You try the present again: it isn't yours.

You buy the rounds and abolish past and present.

When the future smiles you edge away: *don't touch me.*

Late Travellers

Your antiquarian friend
Shows you a perfect city
On its death-bed of water.

October smoke has stolen
Into the dying hair
Of my lover.

He never touches me now.
The curves of my body do not move him.
There is no language for this.

It weighs on me simply, like exhaustion.

Bheir mé o

The night, that traditional
Short-cut, where friendly
Differences meet,
Roving instinctively
In the foot-hallowed places,
The air familiar
And dense and fragrant
As they push it gently nearer
Each other's faces,
Is overgrown by sea
And strangeness now,

A permanent travelling tide
Of long black shadows,
Bright-edged and cold,
Where we, with cancelled senses,
Timidly wade,
Not knowing whose lamp, if any,
Stretches its fingers
In hope or in mimicry
Of hope, from the other side.

The March of the Lance-Bombardier and his Children

The road is stopped with corners; darkness moves
All round us like a forest of blue soldiers.
To walk much farther needs a sense of purpose
Beyond the iron love of feet for world.
There are no villages, not a single cottage.
No lights. Yet everybody takes this road.

The mountains have been blinded and let loose
To wander where they like among the planets.
The waterfalls are only storms of ashes,
The loch a vast slate from the tumbled sky.
No headlamps stare, no burning stubs of cat's-eyes
– And that's why every driver heads this way.

We turned back for the only certain shelter
(Or so we thought) – the one we'd started out from
In flares of sodium, gassy as champagne,
To plunge into the flute-pure black of pine-trees,
Our torch blanching the rain: yes, we turned back,
While you, with ghostly footsteps – you kept walking.

Was it good, sometimes, to march in uniform
In clouds of human breath between the mountains?
Perhaps it almost felt like solitude
With Ursa Major's posed, angular brilliance
Above your head, more pin-up than Great Bear
And other ranks and stragglers, melting nowhere?

You passed us miles ago, we merely saw you
Vanish. Now you must have turned all corners,
Silenced all waterfalls, and reached at last
The garrison town, to wait for further orders.
Something will happen; something always happens.
You steel yourself for the pitching sea-road: France.

Or else you're only dreaming of it all.
Men can nod off, you said, while on the march.
Their eyes close while their feet, on auto-pilot,
Cleave to the old rhythm of the road.
I didn't ask you if they dreamed as well;
But now I'm sure dreams are inevitable.

You lay your kit out by the barracks window;
You brasso every button till it burns
And waters into stars and leafy sunlight.
You swim the green Ardennes; float back, still sleeping;
Begin to darn your heavy, marching sock.
The needle stumbles brightly, pricks your finger.

Your eyes jump up, salute the road again.
All round you is black Scotland, men and pine-trees
Marching as they breathe. Without agreement
Or argument, they haul the sullen load,
And each turned corner pays out a new length
Of dark. Yet everybody takes this road.

Perestroika

This is my sadness
– To have been the future
You thought you wanted.

This is your sadness
– That the most astonishing future
Began without you.

A Meeting of Innocents

A Birthday Sequence

1

On the bus up the hill
She profiles her best side
With its dangling half-moon.

She wouldn't feel unhip
In Carnaby Street: not really.
Her tights said 'Snow-Flake'.

The fishnet holds her nicely:
Small knees, sharp ankles.
Her jacket's PVC.

Getting off on the hill
She's early for the doctor's.
Nufortes is all there is.

Jukebox, burgers, banter,
Manoeuvres. School's out
– But no one even sees her.

That's the only fun
Of being eight months gone.
It shows. You don't.

She crams herself between
Chair-and-table, both
Fixed to the floor, rigid

As the laws of fashion are,
But it's OK, she's in,
Leaning on plastic elbows

To kiss the cappuccino,
Forget the doctor's, feel
How it was to be young

Only a minute ago.

2

The rubber flag tightened
And tightened its clammy grip.
Her heart jumped into her arm

And hammered to get out.
She could almost see her blood
Pulsing round faster than lights

On a neon signboard.
Then the soft, easing sag
And another winding up

With a breathless huff-huff-huff
Like the second climax she'd read
She ought to be capable of.

3

She felt good, she felt perfect
But the needle touched the sky.
It said she was four seas over

And still swallowing –
The child, her toxin.
We'll have to induce. She caught

The name: Pitocin.
They took her in, they sent
A girl nurse to shave her

Without a smile but with
A certain cold finesse.
They frowned at the kitten claw-marks

Pimpling her legs,
Gave her a wooden commode
'To spend a penny in'.

She unclasped the earrings slowly
And lay, inert as her tongue
Over the tasteless drug.

It was the usual thing
After all, being too happy,
Being undone.

4

This was how home slipped through unlucky footsteps,
As the solitary cart of belongings
Tilted into the future by itself;

How the sunrise sank in the eye
Of some huge ocean mammal,
Trussed up and drowned on its back

On blazing boards, its mouth
A stretched, horrified vulva.
The comb of filmy tooth

Would be pliable as fingernails
And laced, she thought, with the green
Last meal of a species.

5

She's living in the novel
That was where she learned about birth
And revolution.

She's not the heroine:
Her ankles are tied
Too far, too wide.

She's got muscles, she must try
To grip the subtext.
She grabs some kind of a mike:

This is an outside broadcast,
I'm here, behind the weather,
The frantic jamming.

Eavesdropping, near to tears,
The poetry-writing doctor
Imagines what it's like.

To live your life
Is not so easy
As to cross a field.

She thinks of Niagara Falls,
Love's second disappointment.
She could scream: but so many

Acres – and in bare feet –
And the mud churning and shifting –
It's easier to live

Your life than to cross this field.
I'm not just crossing the field. I
Am the bloody field.

6

It was the crying hand
Thrust from the shawl, unannounced
As celandines in cold March grass.

It was the five little swimmers,
Waxed in each wrinkle and seam,
Bent at the waist, sea-wearied.

It was the stronghold they shut
Round her probing finger, the way
The crying shivered into stillness,

That made her think that the teeming
Shambles of it all was planned,
And the plan was matchless.

7

They brought her the baby
Every four hours for precisely
Five minutes on each breast.

But the child had travelled too far:
Its lips worked busily
Then slowed, slipped open

In the trance of a lost time-zone.
She could have waited all day,
Conversed with it haltingly

In handfuls of dreamy sucks.
No lover's mouth was exact
Like this, no head so neatly

At rest where her armskin was palest.
But they lifted the child away
And frowned over the scales.

She'll cry later on, they threatened.
Such a thin, inaudible, public
Lament, she thought. The lace cones

Of the nursing-bra turned yellow
And crusty with wastage.
Her arm felt cold. The child

Cried on, somewhere. She cried.
She thought: this is where money starts.
This is how candy's made.

8

She discharged herself politely.
Rode the tall white hospital bus
To her mother's house

– A popcorn maisonette,
Its walls bright-speckled,
Its windows glaring.

Her father came in,
Politely drunk. Withdrawn.
He didn't dislike children

But when, in the kitchen,
She began to unbutton her blouse,
He sent her to her room.

She went out, the high street
Made her dizzy.
She sat in the garden

Among the little rocks
While her husband's mince dinner
Dried out on gas mark three,

The white page in her hand,
On which nothing was written,
Translucent with sunlight.